A THEORY OF CRIMINAL JUSTICE

Jan Gorecki

A THEORY OF CRIMINAL JUSTICE

Columbia University Press • • New York • • 1979

Columbia University Press
New York   Guildford, Surrey

Library of Congress Cataloging in Publication Data

Górecki, Jan.
  A theory of criminal justice.

  Bibliography: p. 165
  Includes index.
  1. Criminal justice, Administration of.
I. Title.
HV8665.G67   364   78-31559
ISBN 0-231-04670-7

TO DANUTA

Contents

vii

53252

CONTENTS

Acknowledgments

THIS IS TO express my thanks to the Rockefeller Foundation for a 1976/1977 Fellowship in Humanities that was most helpful in enabling me to finish the manuscript of this book. I am also grateful to the Center for Advanced Study in the Behavioral Sciences, Stanford, and to the Stanford Law School, for hospitality and excellent facilities during two consecutive summers, 1976 and 1977. My particularly warm thanks go to Solomon E. Asch for discussion of the first, psychological part of the book and to Robert K. Merton for discussion of the section on persuasive communications.

Jan Gorecki

Introduction

CRIMINAL JUSTICE IN the United States is in a state of spreading decay. Crime rates have been rising rapidly in recent decades: reported murder and voluntary manslaughter grew from 4.8 per 100,000 population in 1961 to 8.8 in 1977; forcible rape, from 9.4 to 29.1; robbery, from 58.3 to 187.2; and aggravated assault, from 85.7 to 241.5. This means, in absolute numbers, 19,120 persons murdered in 1977; 63,020 women raped; 404,850 persons robbed; and 522,510 violently attacked;[1] and since, with the exception of murder, the estimated total volume of the crimes committed is about twice as high as of those reported,[2] these numbers should be doubled to reflect truly the scope of criminal behavior in this country.

The direct costs of crime include loss of life and limb, loss of earning capacity by those disabled, physical and mental suffering by the victims and their families, and extensive loss in the victims' property; the aggregate property losses resulting from reported robbery, burglary, and larceny alone exceed $2.5 billion per year.[3]

INTRODUCTION

The indirect costs are more complex. The pecuniary costs include $15 billion a year spent on police, courts, and prisons[4]; expenditure on private guards, detectives, and security devices; defense costs of those accused and, after conviction, welfare assistance for their families; indirect business losses, for example, inflated insurance premiums and loss of business patrons in high-crime areas. (Altogether the estimated direct and indirect economic losses amounted, in 1974, to $90 billion.)[5] What is more unfortunate, however, is a variety of the basically noneconomic indirect costs of crime.

Widespread crime results, first, in widespread fear—a painful and sometimes destructive experience that infringes upon freedom and life habits of those who go through it. They take burdensome precautionary measures, feel compelled to stay off the streets, become distrustful, abandon social contacts, and tend to turn, in a way that atomizes the society, into "mere . . . calculators estimating their . . . own chances for survival amidst their fellows."[6] Such fear contributes, in particular, to the decline of the cities. It does so, first, through the disruption of the social ties—in this case mainly by subdividing a city into "microcosmic communities with loyalty to the immediate neighborhood but hostility and distrust to other areas and their residents."[7] Moreover, it precipitates a flight of the middle class and an outflow of investments from the central parts of the cities, with the resulting loss of city funds, dwindling business, and increasing unemployment and poverty; and the poverty itself results in more criminal behavior and thus closes a vicious circle of crime and urban decline. Since violent crime abounds among minorities, especially in the ghetto, where it victimizes mainly the black and the poor and from where it spreads to other areas, this fear hinders progress in ethnic and race relations. If it were not for fear of crime and violence, then, integration, especially of schools and neighborhoods, would be much easier to achieve. However severe all these harms are, one noneconomic loss seems to be most harmful: the spreading criminality not only results from but also contributes to the progressive moral decline of a large part of the society, especially of an ever-growing segment of the youth. It is no wonder that crime is commonly perceived "as one of the most serious of all domestic problems." [8]

This inquiry intends to discover an optimal policy, for crime control. Various policies have been proposed and tried in this country by criminologists and penal reformers, psychiatrists and psychotherapists, social reformers and revolutionaries. Each group, from the Pennsylvania Quakers to the Marxists and the Freudians, has had an idea, often a hunch suddenly emerging from professional experience or broader ideology, about what makes and unmakes the criminal. These ideas, for the most part too vague ever to be tested, tautological, or evidently false, have been used as premises for action. No wonder that the action has never been very effective.

What is badly needed is not just another hunch but a viable theory. An effort to construct it is presented in the first part of this book. It is a theory that has been deduced from the more general and by now corroborated components of behavioral science. It is specific enough for potential refutation.

The theory concentrates on criminal justice as the most important determinant of criminal behavior. It treats criminal law as an educative tool, or, more precisely, a tool of moral learning by the society at large. If the system of criminal justice is properly arranged, the punished behavior becomes widely perceived as intrinsically wrong and is avoided owing to an intense feeling of its immorality. This is a powerful motivation, much stronger than the fear of sanction. (Of course, criminal justice is not the only determinant of criminal behavior; the others include an almost unlimited number of factors, especially social and psychological. From the standpoint of crime control policy, however, none of these factors matches the importance of criminal justice.)

The theory not only treats criminal law as an implement of learning but also specifies prerequisites for the educative effectiveness of that implement. The specification is followed, in the second part of the book, by an analysis of the system of criminal justice in America. This analysis has been done only to find out whether the system fulfills the prerequisites. The conclusion is that it does not: the system has been developed with an almost total disregard of the educative potential of criminal punishment.

This oversight is an outcome of a double fallacy. First, there is a tendency to overlook the strategic importance of criminal sanctions for controlling crime in favor of other means, such as the discovery and eradication of broader "social causes" of criminal behavior. Secondly, there is a misconception of the role of criminal law even on the part of those who appreciate its importance. They believe that criminal sanctions prevent crime in three major manners: by incapacitating the wrongdoer, by rehabilitating him, and by general deterrence—in the third case, by making potential lawbreakers afraid and thus hindering them from breaking the law. All three avenues, particularly the third, are of use. Nevertheless, use of criminal law as a tool transforming legal prohibitions into moral norms is a much more effective crime control method; indeed, in a civilized society, if crime is not at a very low level, this is the only viable way of preventing criminal behavior. But the method has never been used in the United States; its exclusion eliminated an indispensable implement for crime control and eventually resulted in the present crisis of criminal justice.

The practical implications of the theory and of the analysis of the American scene are clear. The prerequisites for the educative effectiveness of criminal law must be fulfilled. This requires a number of changes in the legal system, outlined in the last part of the book. Once introduced, they should bring about a dramatic decline of criminal behavior.

My book stretches across three disciplines: psychology, sociology, and law. They differ, not only by the structure of the statements they pronounce (the former two aim at constructing theories, whereas the legal science proclaims mainly what ought to be done), but, more importantly, by the technical terminology each uses as its own. Much of the terminology is needed. Often, however, the scholarly sounding technical terms, especially psychological and sociological, constitute hypostases, are invented to cover up ignorance of the objects they denote—"Denn eben wo Begriffe Fehlen da stellt ein Wort zu rechter Zeit sich ein"[9]—or to help make trivia sound like important propositions of scientific knowledge. I shall be unable to avoid using some technical terms, in particular in the first, psychological, part of the book. Their use is, however, limited to the necessary minimum, and their meaning is made as clear as possible; thus, the book is readable for students of all the disciplines involved.

A THEORY OF CRIMINAL JUSTICE

Part One

CRIMINAL JUSTICE AS AN IMPLEMENT
OF LEARNING

Chapter One

LEARNING

CRIMINAL LAW CAN BE applied as an implement of moral education: following a properly arranged application of punishments, the prohibited behavior becomes more forcefully perceived by the society as intrinsically wrong and is avoided as immoral. This creates a motivation clearly superior to fear. Of course, it is nobler; we prefer those who refrain from wrongdoing because of moral aversion. More importantly, it is for several reasons stronger and more reliable. First, fear of sanction prevents crime only as long as the threat operates. Second, even in the presence of the threat, the daring are more effectively prevented from wrongdoing by belief in its immorality than by fear. Furthermore, fear of sanction is the best deterrent only from one portion of criminal behavior—commitment of calculated acts, like professional theft or check forgery; unpremeditated, highly emotional behavior, like killing in a sudden anger, is much less deterrable. On the other hand, internalized aversion effectively prevents both calculated and emotional wrongdoing.

3

CRIMINAL JUSTICE AND LEARNING

The Moral Experience

The assertion that criminal law, if properly arranged, can educate men in society by transforming legal prohibitions into moral norms is not obvious. It takes for granted that moral experiences do exist in our minds. But this runs against the behaviorist stand: its advocates do not admit the existence of moral feelings. In particular the radically oriented behaviorists do not admit the existence of any feelings or any mental experiences at all. They denounce the notions as an invention of the introspective method, and they reject introspection: scientific psychology, like any scientific knowledge, must deal with data open to public scrutiny, while the private interior of human experience is closed to it. Consequently, they either deny the existence of mental experiences or consider any statements of their existence as inadmissible metaphysics. Of course, one cannot claim that punitive contingencies of criminal law may influence moral feelings of the society if those feelings constitute either a myth or metaphysical nonsense.

They constitute neither, however, and we do experience them often and clearly. It was their power that resulted in Socrates' death: his feeling of duty to obey the laws and thus to support Athenian democracy. The feeling of duty to sacrifice one's life for the truth sent Giordano Bruno to the stake. The feeling of disgust and obligation at the famous New Orleans slave market motivated Lincoln's later political actions. These are a few historic instances of the innumerable moral experiences that do emerge in us in response to ideas of conduct that is being evaluated as intrinsically right or wrong (i.e., right or wrong per se, without reference to any purposeful rationale). If the ideas are of present or future conduct, the moral feeling is an experience of duty. For instance, the idea of oneself's or someone else's committing an act of perjury, fraud, or murder causes repulsion: an experience of (my own or someone else's) duty not to do it. The idea of fulfilling a promise or saving a drowning child arouses the feeling of duty toward positive action. If, on the other hand, the ideas are of the past and,

4

moreover, of wrong conduct, the experience of the previously broken duty is known as "guilt": a familiar feeling of one's bad conscience or of someone else's being guilty of wrongdoing. It is exactly this experience of duty that I consider as specifically moral. If it is the feeling of one's own duty, present or future, it has driving properties: it stimulates demanded and inhibits prohibited acts.

For the most part our moral experiences are weak. They emerge as dispositions rather than actual drives and are often below the threshold of consciousness: the majority of us do not steal or cheat, and do pay debts, almost automatically. Counteraction or provocation may, however, make them powerful. If someone counteracts them, for example, tries to persuade us in earnest that we do cheat, commit incest, ridicule in public the disability of a crippled person, or be cruel to someone helpless under our care, our feelings of duty not to do so become clear and strong. Similarly the provocation, such as reading about or witnessing cruelties inflicted by others, arouses the feeling of duty to help the victims and—if the cruelties are committed by nations or governments—the duty to fight a war or a revolution.[1]

It is true that we cannot discover the moral drives without the use of introspection: observing our own mental processes and the body movements resulting from them and inferring contents of the mental processes of others, by analogy, from their body movements. (The body movements include verbal expressions, of course.) It is also true that introspection does not meet the most stringent requirements of testability. Introspective analysis may not, however, be easily abandoned. In the present state of scientific knowledge we do not have any better tool for the discovery of various mental facts, and abandonment of introspection would preclude their exploration at all, in spite of their importance; this is, indeed, what the methodological purism of the behaviorist position requires. Of course, the application of the introspective method must be cautious and critical; it may bring acceptance of only those mental facts that are being experienced obviously, and

5

not just by ourselves but also by qualified others. Hunger, sex, fear, as well as the feeling of duty (which seems to be peculiarly human),[2] are among the most obvious and common facts of experience. Owing to limitations of our knowledge we have been unable to discover any specific neurophysiological indicators for the feeling of duty, and, the more so, to explain it by neurophysiological processes. Perhaps one day the discovery and the explanation will be found. Until then we shall have to be satisfied with introspective understanding.

Whereas a neurophysiological explanation of the moral drives is lacking, their social origin is clear. Each of us acquires them from the society we live in by two partially converging mechanisms: persuasive communications and instrumental learning. I shall discuss each of them in some detail first. Then the moralizing potential of criminal law will become evident.

Persuasive Communications

Communicating about what behavior is right and wrong, about what one should and should not do, occurs in any society with the aid of gestures, facial expressions, example, and especially language. It occurs in individual and group contacts, in particular within symbolic encounters, such as family, religious, judicial, or national ceremonies. This is how "members of a group transmit the evaluations to one another."[3] Thus, each of us acquires evaluations from those with whom we interact: first from parents and childhood peers, then from an increasing number of others. Our peers, both in childhood and in adult life, are particularly influential. Under the impact of their opinion many of us are inclined to believe even in evidently false factual propositions (not to speak of moral judgments, necessarily more ambivalent than statements of fact.)[4] There are also other members of the groups we belong to, especially the individuals we trust and respect: "innumerable studies show that the . . . ethos of a communicator," that is, his "image . . . held in the minds of the receiver(s) . . . is a powerful element in persuasion." [5] We acquire evaluations, moreover, from reference groups—the trusted and respected groups of which we are not members—and from reference individuals, that is; the "public figures who are serving as role models for many." [6]

This process does not fully determine which moral evaluations the majority of us acquire. (I am introducing here the expression "moral evaluation." By this I mean both the perception of which conduct is right or wrong and the experience of duty or guilt emerging in response to ideas of right or wrong conduct.) The evaluations expressed by members of any social group vary, and even in a well-integrated society many of them are in conflict. (For example, is fighting a war in a distant country sometimes right or always wrong? Should abortion be easily accessible, or never, or only occasionally? Should the traditionally underprivileged be given equal or more than equal opportunity of access to scarce goods?) This is why every society—from an illiterate tribe to a modern nation—becomes a large, ongoing "referendum" of evaluations. Some evaluations win the referendum in the process of persuasive communications and become acquired by the majority, while others tend to disappear.

Which evaluations win the referendum? Some functional theorists maintain that all forms of culture, and, among them, moral evaluations and norms, work as adaptive tools: they persist only if they fulfill essential needs of the society and thus serve its "survival." [7] Accordingly, negative evaluations spread in response to behavior harmful for the social group, and positive evaluations, in response to useful behavior. This process goes on without the group members' being necessarily aware of its functional character: they often do not know that their evaluations emerge and spread because of the sometimes very remote social consequences of the behavior they are evaluating. As one functional writer says:

By transmitting . . . evaluations to one another we turn the group into an enormous laboratory of evaluations within which social experience is

7

CRIMINAL JUSTICE AND LEARNING

utilized. Social experience is much richer than the individual, and it takes into account the more distant effects of our actions which are barely accessible to individual experience; for instance, if a member of a primitive tribe perpetrated an act for the first time, for example, killed another tribesman, took his lamb, and invited friends to a mutton feast, there would occur among various partakers in the feast varying appraisals, critical as well as friendly (for example, in the family of the killer, the guests, those unfriendly to the victim). However, the recurrence of killings will eliminate the appraisals which are not conducive to the good of the group, and will strengthen a sharply critical appraisal—thus the killing of a tribesman will be considered a crime. The killing of a member of another group will quickly produce a positive evaluation, and will be perceived as meritorious. In the course of interaction, individual evaluations undergo a process somewhat similar to the struggle for existence and natural selection: those which are not favorable to the group are eliminated, and only evaluations "resultant" from social experience remain—that is, those which are adequate to the social usefulness or harmfulness of the act, and thus serve the group.[8]

In this way innumerable moral evaluations accepted by various societies can be convincingly explained, from the Ten Commandments to the Protestant work ethic to the majority of prohibitions sanctioned by criminal codes of modern democracies—murder, theft, arson, and so on. This self-regulatory process cannot, however, be used as a universal explanation of all moral evaluations (or, even more so, of all forms of culture) that prevail in all societies.

The needs of a society may be understood in either a very broad and vague manner or more specifically. In the first case the just described functional explanation becomes trivial (and sometimes circular): it is always possible to find some vaguely defined "need" served by any widespread evaluation (or cultural pattern).[9] In the more precise understanding, social needs denote various specific adaptive attributes of a society, that is, specific states and processes helping the society to cope with its natural and social environment. Their lists change from one society to another, depending on the problems each of them faces. Thus, for some

8

societies, the list includes the capacity to resist hostility of surrounding nations or to cope with acute internal conflicts, for others, the capacity to cope with plague, famine, or flooding. For some societies speeding up economic or population growth may become a necessity, whereas for others reduction of either may be necessary to, respectively, preserve the natural environment or avoid massive starvation. Since a society is—in the basic, existential meaning of the term *is*—nothing more than an aggregate of individual people (who interact in certain ways), some degree of well-being of the people, and especially avoidance of their widespread suffering, constitutes one attribute that is adaptive for every society; however, the meaning of "well-being" and, to a lesser extent, of "suffering" varies and must be differentially specified for societies standing at different levels of cultural development.[10]

Only this latter, more precise understanding of social needs is acceptable. But its acceptance makes the universal functional explanation false; both history and anthropology provide numerous instances of dysfunctional moral evaluations that did "win the referendum" in many societies—from the evaluations underlying the Inquisition or various religious wars to the ethical components of Nazi ideology.[11] Consequently, the functionalist stand may be approved only with qualification, as a tendency, not a universal truth; moral evaluations that are functional for the society tend to win, whereas those that are dysfunctional tend to disappear. More precisely: the needs of the society are only one social determinant of the spread of moral evaluations.

That this determinant always tends to operate is due to the dependence of each of us on the society we live in, but it may stop working when counteracted by a number of other factors. These others include, in particular, a plurality of conflicting groups within a society: moral evaluations that are functional for any of them may take precedence over those that are functional for the society as a whole.[12] The factors also include an arrest of communications on what is "right" and "wrong," characteristic for tyrannies, especially for modern totalitarian systems. For instance, the Soviet system of pervasive spying, particularly the infiltration of all kinds of groups by informers, renders communication of evaluations on a broad range of issues dangerous. Moreover, the counteracting factors include widespread misinformation, which may come from general ignorance, religious superstitions (like conviction that torture or the stake are needed for the salvation of those possessed by the devil), charismatic demagogues, and, above all, untruths spread by authoritarian rulers (e.g., on wrongdoing or inferiority of the society's neighbors, minorities, dissenters, or on the preferability of the existing political system to all others). Thus, with authoritarianism, ignorance, and internal strife as the most pervasive counteracting forces, chances for the spread of the useful and for the disappearance of the harmful evaluations are best in an open, educated, and well-integrated society.

Instrumental Learning

Instrumental learning provides the second mechanism of moral education. The way instrumental learning works can be deduced from the general truth known as the Law of Effect: behavior of any human (or animal) organism is, to a large extent, an outcome of its likely consequences. Thus, if behavior X brings rewarding, satisfactory effects (sometimes specified as drive reduction due to satisfaction of a need), the organism will tend to repeat X. If, on the other hand, X brings punishing, annoying effects (like displeasure or pain), the organism will tend to avoid X. In other terms: rewarding effects of behavior X reinforce X, while punishing effects reinforce avoidance of X. In this way the Law of Effect accounts for instrumental learning—positive learning following reward, and aversive learning following punishment. (The term *punishment* is being used here, of course, in a much broader meaning than when it is used by criminal lawyers or even in common language: it denotes not only sanction inflicted for an encroachment, but also any, even unintentional, noxious outcome of behavior, for ex-

10

ample burning one's finger after touching fire.) The adaptive character of instrumental learning is obvious: "An organism that . . . remained unresponsive to the outcomes produced by its behavior would enjoy a tragically brief life span."[13]

There are two kinds of instrumental learning: direct and vicarious. The latter is of particular importance for the considerations to follow. It results from observation of behavior of others and its consequences for them; by "observation" I mean here witnessing experiences of both live and pictorial (photographed or filmed) models, as well as reading about or listening to descriptions of other people's experiences. Observation of rewarding consequences enhances similar conduct on the part of the observer, while perceiving noxious effects brings avoidance of the behavior. Experiential data demonstrate that effectiveness of vicarious reinforcers and punishments frequently matches, and sometimes exceeds, that of direct instrumental learning.[14] Moreover, vicarious learning is superior in at least one important respect: it spares us dangers of trial-and-error procedure—a child does not have to be burnt to avoid touching fire.[15]

How does attractive arousal (toward reward-producing behavior) and aversion (from punished behavior) emerge in man? The question is controversial, but we are not in the dark. Preponderant evidence implies that they emerge in two partially interdependent ways. They emerge, first, in the course of a trial-and-error process, owing to more or less "automatic" association of behavior with its immediate consequences, rewarding or noxious; and, second, from an awareness of differential outcomes of our behavior: we become conscious of rewarding or noxious outcomes of behavior X, memorize them, and thus select X or avoidance of X, respectively, for future occasions. The former mechanism has been inherited by us from our animal ancestors, whereas the latter is, at least in its most advanced form, specifically human.[16]

These two adaptive mechanisms—associationist and cognitive—interact. Much human instrumental learning starts as a result of associations operating below the threshold of consciousness,[17]

11

and the subsequent discovery and awareness of rewarding and punishing consequences promote the learning process: "Results of experiments . . . consistently demonstrate that symbolic representation of the conditions of reinforcement has a strong facilitative effect upon overt performance."[18] Vicarious learning involves a somewhat different operation of cognitive and associationist processes. The cognitive process consists of our being conscious of rewarding or noxious. outcomes of behavior X for an observed model, memorizing them, and thus scheduling X or avoiding X for our future conduct. The associationist process works in two ways. As I mentioned earlier, the "observation" denotes both witnessing experiences of others and hearing or reading about them. Witnessing expressions of attractive or aversive emotions by which others respond to rewarding or noxious effects of behavior X may elicit, by empathy, similar emotions on the part of the observer;[19] thus, owing to contiguous association, the observer's emotions become conditioned to the perception of behavior X. Consequently, the imaginal representation of X results in attraction or aversion on the part of the observer.[20] For instance, when a child sees another child touch fire, become burnt, and express pain, the child witnessing the event associates the image of touching fire with the empathetically experienced pain and feels aversion toward similar behavior. Hearing or reading of experiences of others may bring association between the image of X and image of its rewarding or noxious effects, and it is this association or imaginal representations that results in attraction to or aversion from X.[21] For instance, telling a child about someone else's touching fire and experiencing pain often results in association of the touching fire–pain images and aversion on the part of the listener. The two ways—witnessing, as well as hearing or reading—may operate in conjunction: a child may be shown the burnt person in pain and only be told that the person had touched fire; this will evoke association between a verbally elicited image of the dangerous behavior and its witnessed consequences.

There are various prerequisites for efficacy of both direct

12

and vicarious instrumental learning, such as sufficient intensity of reinforcing or punishing events, and their proper timing. In most circumstances the increase in intensity, especially of punishment, makes learning more effective; this is particularly true if punishment is delayed.[22] This general principle will be made more precise and qualified later. The problem of timing is: how quickly should reward or punishment follow behavior X to effectively reinforce or suppress X? The answer varies, depending on the role played by the associative versus cognitive process in evoking attraction or aversion. If attraction or aversion is mainly (or entirely) due to association, the reward or punishment must be quick: a rat should be rewarded or punished seconds after behavior X to reinforce or suppress it.[23] The same seems to hold true with respect to human and infrahuman autonomic responses;[24] punishment of children should sometimes occur at the outset of X to be most effective.[25] If, on the other hand, not only the associative process but also awareness of contingencies strongly mediate the response, speed is less important: when remuneration for work is due in the more distant future, the image of the future reward may get associated with and bring attraction to the work.[26] Similarly, speed is not necessarily crucial for human vicarious learning: an image of reward or punishment may get associated with the image of the rewarded or punished behavior irrespective of whether the behavior had preceded the reward or punishment immediately or some time ago.

Proper scheduling of rewards and punishments is another prerequisite for effective instrumental learning. This prerequisite is most significant for the present considerations. Reward, as well as punishment, may follow behavior X certainly or intermittently. The former means that, whenever X happens, reward follows or, whenever X happens, punishment follows. The latter means that either follows only sporadically: punishment is interspersed with nonpunishment, reward with nonreward, or punishment with reward (e.g., answering a child's tantrums sometimes by hugging and on other occasions by spanking). Moreover, combinations of rewards and punishments often follow this same act (and not only the same kind of behavior). One of them is of particular interest here: punishment following an act that is itself instrumental in bringing reward (e.g., spanking a child after he has eaten prohibited candy or even if he only stretched out hands for it; or having a hangover after drinking liquor). I shall call this combination "punishment of an instrumental response." It is clear that punishment of instrumental responses may also be certain or intermittent: consumption of the liquor may be followed by pain regularly or occasionally.

It is a well-established fact that the two processes just outlined—associationist and cognitive—do operate under the certain scheduling of rewards and punishments; thus, rewards certainly following behavior X bring attraction to X, whereas certain punishments bring aversion from X. This holds true, in particular, with respect to punishment of instrumental responses: if the punishment of a response instrumental in producing reward is certain, it brings aversion, provided that it is strong enough to overwhelm the reward.

Do the two processes operate under intermittent schedules and, if so, how effectively? One might guess that intermittent rewards following X bring at least some attraction toward X and thus operate as reinforcers, but the reinforcement is weaker than that brought by regular rewards. Analogically, one might guess that intermittent punishments following X bring at least some aversion that would not have emerged if there had been no punishment at all, but the aversion is weaker than that brought by certain punishment.

Neither of the two guesses is correct, however. It has been discovered by Humphreys and corroborated by many others that intermittent rewards reinforce behavior more effectively than regular ones. To be sure, intermittent rewards operate somewhat slower, but, once rewards end, behavior that had been intermittently rewarded, especially on a variable schedule,[27] persists longer than behavior rewarded each time it had occurred.[28] (This

14

does not contradict at least some of our commonsense knowledge: Las Vegas gamblers try persistently through long periods of losing, and adults who had been rewarded only intermittently in childhood are often, in unrewarding circumstances, more persistent, stronger persons than those who had been "spoiled" by continuous rewards.) On the other hand, whereas certain punishment brings aversion, intermittent punishment.of an instrumental response does, rather unexpectedly, reinforce the punished behavior, not suppress it. The response that had been intermittently punished is more resistant to elimination (by subsequent certain punishment) than behavior that had never been punished at all.

This inferiority of intermittent punishment in producing aversion finds some corroboration in various nonexperimental studies: delinquency has been found correlated to capricious parental discipline,[29] and intermittent punishments that had been applied to extinguish children's dependent behavior apparently increased its strength.[30] More importantly, the inferiority has been clearly demonstrated in numerous experiments on humans and on.animals alike.[31] It holds, however, within certain limits only: if intermittent punishment is so powerful as to produce truly shocking aversion, it may have permanent suppressive quality even if it happens only a few times or once.[32]

How to explain the superiority of intermittent rewards in arousing attraction and the inferiority of intermittent punishments in arousing aversion? Again, two inseparable processes account for this. One of them, the cognitive, works in man more forcefully than in animals. Regularly rewarded subjects quickly lose hope and become disappointed once rewards disappear, whereas those rewarded intermittently are not sure that there will be no more rewards and thus continue trying; and subjects whose instrumental responses are followed by intermittent punishment often feel that it pays to risk an occasional punishment. This cognitive process works under directly as well as vicariously experienced rewards and punishments; as I said earlier, observers who become conscious of the outcomes of the model's behavior for him schedule

15

their future conduct as if they had been directly rewarded or punished.

The second process is associationist and operates forcefully in both man and animals. Amsel was the first to convincingly use it as an explanation for the superiority of intermittent rewards.[33] Nonreward that follows behavior X after some rewarded trials is frustrating: it operates like mild punishment. However, since the nonreward is followed, sooner or later, by rewards, the experience of nonreward becomes a signal for the impending rewards; in other words, the experience of nonreward becomes a classically conditioned stimulus reinforcing X and, consequently, making X more resistant to extinction. An extension of this account to punishment explains the inferiority of intermittent punishment. If behavior X is followed by occasional rewards interspersed with occasional punishments, the intermittent punishment of X becomes a signal for the impending rewards and does, as a classically conditioned stimulus, reinforce X[34] (provided that the punishment is not as powerfully shocking as to completely extinguish X after a few trials or at once).

The same explanation holds with respect to intermittent punishment of an instrumental response: the punishment becomes a cue for the impending nonpunished reinforcements and, as a classically conditioned stimulus, makes X more persistent. Again, this associationist process works, not only under directly, but also under vicariously experienced rewards and punishments. Because of the general impact of vicarious experiences on observers, intermittent nonreward of a model's behavior (under intermittent reward schedule) and intermittent punishment of his instrumental responses become signals stimulating similar behavior on the part of the observer.

The inferiority of intermittent punishment in arousing aversion is an issue of utmost importance for the moral learning, to which I will return soon. First, however, one other important question requires elucidation. This is the differential character of attractions and aversions aroused, respectively, by rewards and punishments.

I have been speaking indiscriminately about instrumentally learned attractions to and aversions from various kinds of behavior, as if all the attractions were alike and all the aversions were alike. But introspective analysis makes it clear that neither are uniform: attractions to, as well as aversions from, various kinds of behavior constitute very different experiences. (This also holds true with respect to noninstrumentally learned and innate attractions and aversions.) For instance, the feeling of attraction that drives an addict to drug use differs from the curiosity that drives a researcher to spend nights at a laboratory. The urge of an inmate to get out of jail, of a girl to buy a new dress, of a believer to go to church, or of a cuckolded husband to take revenge are other instances of attractions with differing ''emotive tone.'' Aversions are equally diversified. Some are nauseating, like disgust experienced at the sight of decayed meat or worms in one's meal. They evidently differ from the feelings that prevent us from breaking good manners—picking one's nose or undressing at a formal dinner. Anyone's suggestion that we gouge out an animal's eyes brings, again, a very different feeling of aversion. Still another is the fear that prevents us from toying with explosives. All these differences among attractions and among aversions can be easily discovered by introspection (and, to make this clear, I included a few strong instances here). Moreover, objective observation often supports the discovery; for instance, body movements and physiological processes of someone repelled from eating decayed food are unlike those of a person overwhelmed by fear.

Persuasive Instrumental Learning of Moral Experiences

A satisfying or noxious stimulus can be explicitly arranged to follow behavior X. Thus arranged, it is called, respectively; ''re-

17

ward'' and ''punishment'' in the common language, in a meaning much narrower than that in which I have been using the two terms thus far.[35] In a still narrower and particularly important meaning, reward can be made explicitly contingent upon a behavior evaluated as intrinsically right, and punishment can be made explicitly contingent upon a behavior evaluated as intrinsically wrong. This is how, in general, parents or schools reward children for acts of sacrifice or helpful courage and punish them for lying or cheating. This is how the army responds to similar acts of soldiers, and various churches to the acts of their members. The rewards and punishments vary: gifts and culinary treats, honors and promotions, the promised salvation, acknowledgment and friendliness on the part of the rewarding agents are among the former; the latter include verbal rebuke and spanking, loss of rights, privileges and honors, constraints of freedom, future pains in hell, withholding affection, and the like. All of them have one common characteristic: when applying them, the rewarding or punishing agent makes it clear that they are being applied for behavior that ought to have been done as intrinsically right or ought to have been avoided as intrinsically wrong. Consequently, their application works in a dual process: as an implement of persuasive communication and an implement of instrumental learning or, briefly, as an implement of ''persuasive instrumental learning.'' Thus, if effectively applied, they bring attractions and aversions with peculiar emotive tone: a feeling of duty to do what is right, and a feeling of duty to avoid wrongdoing. This is how, owing to the persuasive instrumental learning, moral experiences are acquired—or, in other terms, moral norms get internalized.[36]

The acquisition is brought about by both kinds of persuasive instrumental learning—direct and vicarious. Sometimes the former prevails, for example, in parental upbringing of an only child, but, on the whole, the latter is much more widespread. It prevails among siblings in a large family, schoolchildren, boy scouts, and in army units, where every member of the group observes rewards awarded to many others for right behavior and punishments imposed on them for wrongdoing. The same holds true in various religious groups: none of their members has ever directly experienced the delights of paradise or the suffering in hell, but many do so vicariously when reading various scriptures or horrors by Dante.

What are the prerequisites of effectiveness for persuasive instrumental learning of moral experiences, direct and vicarious? There are many, for example, motivational dispositions of the learner, proper intensity of rewards and punishments, and their timing. Two of them are, however, crucial for this writing. The first, essential for any instrumental learning, is the intermittence of rewards and certainty of punishments—and the preceding general discussion of the issue is fully relevant here. The second, essential for any persuasive communications, is exactly their persuasiveness—an issue that, besides the general discussion, requires a few more specific comments now.

To make of a reward a moral communication that is persuasive, the beneficiary must be impressed that he is being rewarded because his behavior was intrinsically right, and so must be observers who experience vicarious reinforcement. To make of a punishment a moral communication that is persuasive, the punished subject must be impressed that he is being punished because his behavior was intrinsically wrong, and so must be the observers. This can be effectively done only under two conditions. First, the rewarded behavior must be widely experienced as right in the social group, and the punished behavior as wrong. If a school principal rewards a student for cheating or punishes him for candor, it will impress neither the culprit nor observers that the behavior is being rewarded because it was right or punished because it was wrong. Second, the reward or punishment must be, in all other respects, just. If a principal punishes only the single ethnic student for an act committed also by all other members of the class, or if he applies an extremely harsh measure for petty encroachment, he will impress no one that the behavior is being punished because it was wrong. To be sure, unjust rewards or punishments of any behavior can result in attraction to or aversion from it, especially owing to awareness of the impending benefits or to fear of sanction. The attraction or aversion will, however, be void of the specifically moral emotive tone: having no persuasive moral power, the rewards and punishments cannot bring about the experience of duty.

Some characteristics of the rewarding and punishing agent constitute another condition influencing the persuasiveness: he should be respected and trusted. As I have mentioned above, any moral communications are most persuasive if they come from those whom we trust and respect. This is particularly true if rewards and punishments are being applied as moral communications: the moral condemnation by punishment that comes from an unjust and despised school principal or army commander will hardly impress anyone, even if it happens to be deserved. On the other hand, it will impress the culprit and observers when coming from someone admired for his integrity—its persuasive power may sometimes even be strong enough to alleviate doubts whether, in a given case, the punishment itself is just.[37]

To conclude this analysis one more comment is necessary. In the foregoing paragraphs I have been speaking of justice: rewards and punishments must be just to make the moral communications persuasive, and so must be the rewarding and punishing agents themselves. The terms *just* and *justice* are, however, among the most ambiguous: followers of various systems of normative ethics—Socratic, utilitarian, Marxist, Nietzschean, or others—understand them differently. Therefore clarification of the meaning in which they have been used in the preceding passages is needed.

What do we mean when saying: "This schoolboy is being punished by his principal justly" or "This principal is a just person" or "Norm X pronounced by the principal is just"? We refer such statements to acts or character of, or to norms pronounced by, those in power who distribute rewards and punishments, goods and burdens.[38] When making the first assertion we mean that a person in power has performed a distribution in a way that we evaluate as morally right: we experience his duty to perform it in this way. When making the second, we mean that a person in power always makes distributions that we evaluate as morally right. When making the last, we mean that a norm enacted by a powerholder orders a distribution that we evaluate as morally right. Thus, any society or social group calls a distribution of rewards or punishments "just" if the distribution matches moral experiences prevailing in the group, and it calls a person in power "just" if he continuously performs the just distributions. In this meaning the term *justice* is metaethical: its use does not imply adherence to any particular system of normative ethics.

Since moral sentiments of various societies differ, the same distribution may be just in one society and unjust in another. There is a limitation to this variability, however: one moral demand referring to the distributions seems to be constant. This is the claim that each distribution be made according to uniform criteria and not capriciously. For instance, if severity of punishments for a prohibited behavior depends upon whims, prejudices, or personal interests of the punishing agents, the punishments will run against the moral sentiment of any society. Thus, acceptance of uniform criteria—"a uniform or constant feature, summarized in the precept 'Treat like cases alike' "[39]—is a universal prerequisite for just distributions.[40] I shall call this prerequisite "consistency," and rewards or punishments distributed according to uniform criteria "consistent rewards" and "consistent punishments." Consistency is a necessary condition for the justice of any distribution but, of course, not a sufficient one: to be just, a consistent distribution must match all other relevant moral requirements that, changing from one society to another, do prevail in the society where the distribution is being made. For instance, a norm making severity of punishment for crimes dependent upon income—the poorer a criminal, the harsher the punishment—provides a uniform criterion enabling judges to inflict consistent punishments. However, the resulting distribution would run against the moral sentiment of—and thus be unjust in—any democratic society. All this leads to "a certain complexity in the structure of the idea of justice." [41] To be just, the distributions must always, under any system, be consistent, that is, just with respect to one another. Moreover, each of them must be in accord with the current, historically engendered moral code of a given society.

Criminal Law as an Implement of Moral Learning

This chapter has clear implications for criminal justice: all the above propositions on the functioning of punishment in general specifically refer to the addressees of criminal punishment. This is particularly true of the propositions on the instrumental learning of moral experiences.

Who are the addressees? The direct addressee is the criminal himself, but, for reasons I mention later, making his moral education the main purpose of a criminal justice system can easily result in destruction of the system itself. [42] It is the indirect addressee—the society at large—that constitutes the proper audience for moral education through criminal sanctions. All of us, especially potential lawbreakers, can acquire moral experiences by process of vicarious learning—observation of criminals being punished for the crimes.

The prerequisites of effectiveness for the moral learning of this kind can be deduced from the preceding general account of the persuasive instrumental learning. The first prerequisite, characteristic of all aversive instrumental learning, is certainty of punishment. Perfect certainty of criminal punishment means that every crime is punished. This is an ideal that cannot be fully achieved (on which, again, I elaborate later). However, its approximation is essential. In any society, and especially in an open society of today, punishment of criminals is easy to perceive by its members. Some of the members—criminal lawyers and law enforcement officers, fellow convicts, press and television reporters—witness

22

53252

punishment of live models. The vast majority witness pictorial presentations of suffering of punished criminals and read and hear about it. If punishment is applied certainly, this vicarious experience does, owing to the psychological processes described earlier, arouse aversion. If punishment is intermittently applied, it is counterproductive; since criminal behavior is most often itself instrumental in bringing various rewards, its intermittent punishment vicariously reinforces criminal behavior. There is one exception to this, however: vicarious punishment of extreme power, like the immediately observed or televised death of a culprit under elaborate torture, can inhibit the punished behavior after a few trials or even at once.[43]

The second prerequisite is that criminal punishment be persuasive as moral communication. This implies that the punishment must be imposed for behavior widely experienced as wrong, must be in all other respects just, and must be imposed by respected and trusted agents. In discussing these conditions, I shall, with some oversimplification, deal with the first two under the common heading of "justice," because justice of a criminal punishment largely presupposes wrongfulness of the punished behavior.[44]

In the understanding of justice accepted here, criminal punishments are just if they match the feeling of justice of the society where they are being imposed. The "matching" means a conjunction of three requirements, all of them implied in the foregoing comments: the punishments must be imposed for justly selected kind of behavior, they must be applied consistently, and their severity must be just.

The first requirement limits infliction of punishments to behavior that, in the dominant opinion, not only is wrong but should be punished. I assume here that in most societies there is at least basic consensus on what kinds of wrongdoing deserve criminal punishment. The assumption does not claim full uniformity of evaluations of what is right and wrong; it only claims a prevailing agreement on some minimal demands of acceptable behavior that must be enforced. The assumption holds true, not only in tradi-

23

tional homogeneous groups, but also in highly complex, pluralistic societies like ours. There is, for instance, almost full consensus in the United States that violence against persons should be punished, whereas criticizing the government should not.

The second requirement is that punishments be consistent: they must be applied according to uniform criteria, not arbitrarily. Thus, if A and B committed like crimes in like circumstances, and A gets sentenced to life imprisonment, whereas B is incarcerated only for a brief term, the requirement is not being met; nor is it if A gets convicted and B goes free. (In the latter case, inconsistency converges with infringement of certainty of punishment.) Finally, the severity of the consistently applied punishments must be just. It is not, if it is at odds with the actual, historically engendered moral sentiment of the society—especially if the punishments are perceived as a cruel kind of response to any crime or as a response too severe for the crime committed. Here again, I assume that in most societies there is some basic consensus on just severity of punishments. For example, there is little doubt in the United States that torture is always unjustly severe, even if inflicted consistently for the most heinous offenses; that life imprisonment would be unjustly severe if consistently imposed for shoplifting; or that 20 years is too much for a joy ride. True, the consensus is not always there: views of any society on proper severity of penalties evolve,[45] and occasionally an emerging change of the views brings sharp dissent. For instance, the slowly changing views on capital punishment in this country have resulted in a division of opinion, the majority sometimes favoring and sometimes opposing the death penalty.[46] (This uncertain stand has been reflected by a hesitation of the lawmakers and of the Supreme Court whether to retain or to abolish it.) Furthermore, wherever a wide consensus on severity of punishment exists, it is rarely a consensus on the very precise measure determining exactly how severe a penalty should be. It is rather a feeling that, from some point on, the punishment becomes intolerably severe (or intolerably lenient), as the cited instances of penalties for shoplifting or for a joy ride should make clear.

CRIMINAL JUSTICE AND LEARNING

This last issue—the severity of punishments as a source of injustice—constitutes a traditional dilemma under various legal systems. It is so because many lawmakers and courts consider general deterrence—the vicariously aroused fear of punishment—as the main or even exclusive purpose of criminal law. Accordingly, criminal punishment should be severe enough to arouse effective fear—either exactly severe enough or harsher than that. From this standpoint punishments perceived by the society as excessively harsh, even cruel, also make a useful tool. Thus, lawmakers and judges of this orientation are often tempted to impose excessively harsh measures, the more so that the demand for punishments severe enough to arouse effective fear is vague; few, if any, of them are able to determine how severe is exactly severe enough.

If general deterrence were the basic purpose of criminal law, this would be a legitimate stand. Replacement of the deterrence by moral education makes the stand fallacious. An excessively harsh punishment is unjust and, therefore, both its enactment on the criminal code and its infliction by criminal courts are void of persuasive moral power. Worse than that, they seem to be counterproductive: "Seeing inequitable punishment may free incensed observers from self-censure of their own actions, rather than prompting compliance, and thus increase transgressive behavior."[47] In the words of a most keen observer written long ago: "If the society considers a penalty as unjustly harsh, its application . . . brings sympathy and friendliness for the offender." These feelings may easily become, owing to an association of images, "extended to the prohibited acts themselves; which undermines disgust for crime and, sometimes, even results in glorifying the criminal and in favoring harmful behavior."[48] At the same time, by generating resentment in the society, excessively harsh punishments "undermine the legitimacy" of the punishing agents[49]—respect for and trust in them—and thus further erode the persuasive power of criminal justice.

The respect and the trust are another condition for the persuasiveness. Both direct and indirect punishing agents—criminal lawmakers and criminal courts—must be respected and trusted.

25

Prestige of the lawmakers depends mainly on their integrity and, especially, on the just character of the norms they enact. These qualities are, to a large extent, predetermined by the political system of a society. For obvious reasons they are present rather in open societies than in tyrannies. Subject to political checks, the democratic lawmakers are at least prevented from too much wrongdoing, in particular from enacting laws that run very clearly against the general moral sentiment. Prestige of courts means respect for and trust in those who decide criminal cases—professional judges, lay judges, jurors, and the like. The respect for and trust in them depend, again, upon their integrity and, especially, upon the just character of the decisions they deliver.

The respect and trust have persuasive influence of their own, partially independent of the just character of a particular norm or decision. This means that the high prestige of criminal lawmakers increases the persuasive power of a just criminal norm and that the high prestige of a criminal court increases the persuasiveness of a just punishment the court inflicts. Moreover, their high prestige may, to a limited degree, alleviate doubts whether a given norm or a given decision is, indeed, just.[50] On the other hand, as the present analysis should make clear, prestige of criminal lawmakers results predominantly from the just character of the norms they enact, and the prestige of criminal courts, from the just character of the decisions they pronounce. Consequently, the prestige is, to a large extent, explainable by, and in this sense reducible to, the general requirement of justice. That is why, in the following comments, I discuss the prestige within that general requirement, and not separately.

In conclusion, criminal law can be an effective implement of moral learning. Of course, it may not be treated as the only implement. Even more so, it may never be perceived as the only or the main source of morality in any society. As the preceding analysis should make clear, the sources of any society's moral sentiment are complex, and learning by criminal sanctions constitutes but one of them. Moreover, the sanctions are always a "second-

26

ary'' source: to be morally effective, a sanction must be imposed for behavior widely experienced as morally wrong. In spite of these obvious limitations, criminal sanction can constitute a powerful implement, and the implement may be used in a relatively easy manner—an issue to which I shall return later.

The statement of the moralizing power of criminal law is not new: it was hinted long ago by Bentham,[51] accepted by Petrazycki[52] and several others.[53] In Durkheim's view, "the essential function of punishment is not to make the guilty expiate his crime through suffering or to intimidate possible imitators through threats, but to buttress . . . consciences";[54] and even Socrates considered the law of Athens as a teacher of virtue. However, in the words of Andenaes, the statement is made "with great confidence, but there does not seem to be much research or practical experience to substantiate" it.[55] An effort to substantiate it has been made here: the statement has been deduced from the otherwise corroborated elements of the behavioral science. Granted veracity of the elements and validity of the deduction, not only is the statement true, but also the basic prerequisites for the effectiveness of the educative power of criminal law are clear. They are just and certain application of criminal punishments. Both should be present in a well-arranged system of criminal justice.

Are they present in the American system? Is behavior to be punished justly selected? Are punishments consistent and of just kind and measure? How certain is their infliction? These questions are discussed in the following chapters. To answer them, I deal with justice first and then with the difficult dilemma of certainty.

Part Two

CRIMINAL PUNISHMENT IN AMERICA

Chapter Two

JUSTICE

HERETICS WERE TORTURED and burnt alive under the laws of the Inquisition. Being a Jew or hiding a Jew was a capital crime in Nazi-occupied Europe. Being a kulak or having contact with foreigners was sanctioned by 25 years of hard labor in Stalinist camps—a penalty that only relatively few survived. No open society would tolerate such contradictions between legal norms and practices, and widespread moral feelings. Even in democracies, however, discrepancies emerge. They emerge in the United States on all the three issues determining the justice of criminal punishment: the selection of behavior to be punished, severity of punishments, and their consistency.

It would be difficult for the American lawmakers, who depend directly on the electorate, to make a selection running clearly against the dominant moral sentiment. However, the moral sentiment on what kinds of behavior should be punished evolves, whereas legal norms easily become fixed and difficult to change. That is why penalties for some acts, introduced into the law long ago and then perceived as morally right, are becoming obviously unjust today. It would be even more difficult for the lawmakers to enact intolerably severe penalties: their introduction would not only be politically inexpedient, but it might also run against the Eighth Amendment's ban on cruel and unusual punishments. Under its well-established construction, the ban operates irrespective of whether the severity makes the punishment totally intolerable or only intolerably harsh for the crime committed.[1] In spite of these safeguards, cruel criminal penalties are being inflicted in America. Conditions in many prisons (and jails) are the most conspicuous instance here, especially physical abuse of prisoners by fellow convicts—beating, stabbing, homosexual assaults, and individual and group rapes of younger inmates. The violence makes the punishment brutal, and even though the brutality is not intended by prison administration, the administration is to blame. Providing for basic physical security of inmates constitutes, despite some distressingly ambiguous court decisions,[2] an obvious obligation of any penal institution.

However serious all this is, inconsistency of punishments amounts to the most frequent and, as we shall see, most harmful kind of injustice. Oddly enough, it sometimes starts with lawmakers who occasionally enact penalties "not on any systematic basis but rather by according [their] ad hoc attention to some discrete area of criminality in which there is a current hue and cry. Distinctions are thus drawn which do not have the slightest bearing on the relative harmfulness of conduct"[3] or any other meaningful criterion.[4] More importantly, sweeping and often unchecked discretionary powers are given to those who process individual cases, in particular to the police, prosecutors, judges, and parole boards. The "law in action" governing police behavior has departed far away from the norms on the books of various states and localities. According to the norms it is the duty of the police to fully enforce criminal statutes by apprehending known criminals. In fact, police have discretionary power not to arrest them, and thus to preclude punishment, even if the crime can easily be proved. The power is exercised "without review . . . without stating reasons, and without relating one case to another"[5]—a clear violation of consistency (which converges with an infringement of certainty of punishment).

Once the decision to arrest has been made by the police, the sweeping discretionary powers pass onto prosecutors and judges. They exercise the powers, in particular, under the guise of plea bargaining. Moreover, judges fix sentences in an unchecked way within very broad statutory boundaries; and, when indeterminate sentences are stipulated by the law, parole boards are free to keep the convict in prison as long as they feel proper or to release him whenever they want to. Many lower courts, overburdened as they are, fix penalties without learning the facts of the case and without acquiring evidence.

All this results in an arbitrariness of proportions unknown to any other open society. Clearly, the list of injustices is long. I chose a few particularly impressive items from the list and shall discuss them now. The first two—penalties for homosexual behavior and for drug addiction—consist of a wrong selection of punishable behavior. The other—judicial sentencing powers, indeterminate sentences, and plea bargaining—consist of sweeping discretion, a resultant arbitrariness, and, at least in one kind of cases, cruelty of punishments.

Wrong Selection of Punishable Behavior: Homosexual Acts

Various acts are made criminal in the United States that should not be punished according to the moral sentiment of one or another group. There are a few acts whose punishment runs against the dominant moral values, that is, is unjust in the here accepted meaning of "justice." Punishment of two of them—homosexual behavior and drug abuse by addicts—is· particularly unjust.

Homosexual behavior between consenting adults in private

33

is a criminal offense in 44 of the states. It is a classical instance of a "victimless crime." The expression is being used in America to denote a variety of criminal behavior. The (not unanimously accepted[6]) list includes—besides homosexuality—gambling, drug abuse, prostitution, abortion, and a number of less frequently prosecuted crimes, like attempted suicide, vagrancy, or fornication. What is their common characteristic? According to an often expressed view, they do not harm anyone: nobody, at least nobody other than the criminal himself, suffers from them, but they are prohibited and punished despite their harmlessness.

Reasons for the original introduction of the prohibitions and punishments differ. Prohibition of vagrancy was implemented because of the need to persuade medieval men to work,[7] and for economic interests of powerful groups.[8] The ban on gambling was a corollary of the Puritan stand: "man should prosper . . . only by means of his own efforts, and not through the sheer intervention of chance or providence."[9] Moreover, the ban has been supported by a belief that gambling, even if legalized, falls unavoidably under the control of racketeers and brings widespread fraud and political corruption.[10] Punishment of drug abuse, which emerged in the wake of the Harrison Act of 1914, resulted from mixed motives: belief in criminogenic properties of narcotics, their harmful impact on the user's ability to work, and a paternalistic concern about the user's good. Other prohibitions, for example, the ban on suicide or fornication, emerged mainly because of religious doctrines. This was especially true of homosexual behavior: contempt for it has been derived from the Bible[11] and reinforced by the Puritan influence. It was clearly mediated by the British law, where sodomy had been a capital crime from the sixteenth century until 1891.[12]

Some of the prohibitions were apparently instrumental in the past—like the ban on vagrancy for the economic progress of medieval England, or the ascetic, Puritan prohibitions in the young, undeveloped America, immersed in the struggle for rapid economic growth. All of them were, at the time of their introduction, either supported by dominant moral sentiment or at least not widely opposed. Today, however, the support for some of them is waning and the opposition grows: before our eyes they are becoming obviously unjust. This is particularly true of homosexual behavior. Why?

The spread of liberal and utilitarian moral views in the United States, at the expense of the rigidly Puritan stand, provides the explanation. This spread became feasible in a society where the work ethic became strongly imbedded and brought tangible economic effects; the affluent society has been able to shift from the moral rule of ascetic pioneers to a more flexible code of ultimate values. Liberalism stresses freedom as the ultimate value. Utilitarianism stresses promotion of the general welfare or, more precisely, avoidance of harm and suffering. A combination of the two seems to be a dominant and ever-growing influence in America today; everyone should be free to do whatever he wants, as long as it does not harm others. The implications of this moral stand for criminal justice are obvious. No behavior, even if widely perceived as morally wrong, should be prohibited or punished unless it harms others.[13] The idea had been expressed long ago by John Stuart Mill: ''The only purpose for which power can be rightfully exercised over any member of a civilised community, against his will, is to prevent harm to others.''[14]

The idea cannot be accepted without reservation, however. Some limitations may and should be imposed on individuals for their own good. Mill himself acknowledged paternalist prohibitions protecting children and the insane. Today, even with respect to sane adults, legal ''paternalism—the protection of people against themselves—is a perfectly coherent policy''[15] if pursued with restraint, to avoid great and obvious dangers. The majority of us would not object to norms that require that motorcyclists use safety helmets, and automobile drivers, safety belts, nor would we regard mild punishments sanctioning those norms as immoral.[16] With this reservation, the currently dominant moral stand is: the law should never prohibit anyone from, or punish him for, behavior that is neither harmful to others nor can be greatly harmful to himself. The implications of this stand for homosexual behavior are clear: if it does not harm anyone—neither others nor the homosexual—its prohibition and punishment are unjust and should be removed from the criminal codes of this country.

Is it, indeed, harmless? Certainly not, if it is committed with a minor; by use of force, threat, or fraud; or in public. However, it would be difficult to discover any harm for anybody resulting from homosexual behavior between consenting adults in private. In particular, it is impossible to accept the argument of those who believe in its unlimited spreading power: they predict that decriminalizing homosexual acts committed in private would " 'open the floodgates' and result in unbridled license," [17] leading to degeneration and decay of the society. [18] The prediction assumes that the general attractiveness of homosexual behavior "would impel hordes of individuals . . . to discard their current heterosexual inclinations . . . for a life of homosexuality, thus precipitating the decline . . . of the conventional family and of civilization as we know it." [19] One could add that the whole society might die off as a result of the demise of heterosexual interest. All these harms are pure fantasy, of course, easy to rebut by the experience of the numerous European countries where homosexual acts between consenting adults in private have long been off the list of criminal offenses.

Thus, since homosexual behavior does not harm anyone, even if it is widely perceived as wrong or unaesthetic, [20] its prohibition and its punishment are, from the standpoint of the actually accepted basic moral values, unwarranted. Only the lack of knowledge of its harmlessness explains why the proportion of those who support the prohibition and the punishment is considerable. The knowledge is, however, spreading, and the number of supporters shrinks. In 1965, 70 percent, and in 1969, 63 percent of Americans believed in its harmfulness. [21] In 1970 the majority of the total adult population was still in favor of its punishment, but the majority was not overwhelming: it amounted to 59 percent. This was,

36

moreover, in part, a confused and hesitant majority; many of its members felt, rather inconsistently, that what consenting adult homosexuals do in private "is no-one else's business."[22] In 1977 the majority disappeared: those for and against the punishment were equally divided.[23] Knowledge of the harmlessness, and the ensuing contempt for the prohibition and punishment, are, of course, most widespread among those well educated. Thus, only 16 percent of a sample of university students interviewed in 1962 opted for punishment.[24] Antipunitive sentiment was expressed by the majority of the medical profession.[25] A leading group of legal draftsmen recommended decriminalization, as early as 1955, in the Model Penal Code, and a similar recommendation was adopted in England, by the Wolfenden Committee, in 1957[26] (and enacted by the Parliament in 1966).[27] A Task Force on Homosexuality at the National Institute of Mental Health accepted, in 1969, an identical stand.[28] Among judges, "there seems to be a reluctance . . . to impose stringent sanctions."[29] A growing number of writers—scholars, politicians, journalists—are joining the antipunitive campaign. Owing to the change in the general moral climate, the spread of specific knowledge of harmlessness of homosexual behavior, and the influence of all the groups just mentioned, the prohibition and punishment of homosexual acts between consenting adults in private are becoming clearly unjust in the United States.

The prohibition brings a particularly painful limitation of liberty: "The homosexual . . . has no legal outlet for the kind of sex life to which he is drawn; his only alternative to lawbreaking is abstinence."[30] This alternative means a permanent "suppression of sexual impulses."[31] If he does not conform, he risks conviction. Two further circumstances increase the hardship. First, law enforcement procedures—involving frequent enticement, or even entrapment, by police decoys—are humiliating,[32] and so is the trial itself; it is often "a trial by smear, not a trial by jury."[33] Second, the threat of punishment brings unintended side-effects that aggravate the suffering; homosexuals are often exposed to blackmail, extortion, and violence.[34] All these miseries—imposed on those whose sexual inhibition makes them suffer anyway, irrespective of the cruelty of the law—are largely responsible for the fact that "depressive and suicidal reactions . . . occur much more often among those with homosexual tendencies."[35]

Homosexual behavior is only one of a number of victimless crimes.[36] Few of them are, however, as harmless, and with respect to none (except drug abuse by addicts[37]) are the prohibition and punishment as cruel. One consequence of the injustice is that it makes the punishment morally unpersuasive and thus void of educative influence. There is nothing particularly troublesome about this; it is not the law's business to persuade the society that a harmless behavior is morally wrong. The other consequence is, however, much worse. The unjust sanctions undermine the society's belief in the justice of the legal system, especially of the lawmakers and the courts. The consequent decline of their prestige diminishes the moral persuasiveness of other punishments they impose, however well deserved all those punishments may be, and thus undermines the general educative power of criminal law.

Wrong Selection of Punishable Behavior: Drug Abuse

By "drug abuse" I understand here illegal use of psychoactive drugs. Most of them fall into three categories: depressants, stimulants, and hallucinogens. The depressants include narcotics— opiates and their synthetic substitutes—which account for the major part of drug addiction in the United States; and heroin, the most powerful of them, accounts for more than 90 percent of all illicit use.[38]

Abuse of drugs is usually considered another victimless crime. This is not quite correct, however, if a "victimless crime" means a harmless criminal offense. Drug abuse is often harmful to the user himself and to others. The harms vary, depending, especially, on the kind of drug, the dose, and the frequency and regularity of administration. Opiates, and especially heroin—by far the most widely abused drug in America—bring a number of unfortunate effects. First, their use results in severe dependence. In general, they act in a satisfying manner on the central nervous system, bringing relief of pain, freedom from anxiety, and euphoria—a strong, generalized feeling of well-being. All these gratifications, normally achieved through socially valuable and demanding activities, are being acquired without effort, easily, by a simple shot; that is why the persons who are unable to perform activities successfully—socially handicapped people, neurotics, psychopaths— are particularly addiction prone.[39] The continued use of opiates results in a quickly growing tolerance—an adaptive change in the central nervous system that renders the user less sensitive to the drug.[40] Consequently, ever-increasing doses must be used to achieve the rewarding effects. Dependence occurs after a short period of continued use; in the process of instrumental learning, there emerges an intense craving for the drug. While the rewarding effects, especially euphoria, work as positive reinforcers, a negative reinforcer additionally strengthens the drive. If the drug is withheld, the central nervous system, already adapted to continued use, reacts with excessive responsiveness to normal stimuli. The ensuing withdrawal reaction is severe.[41] As a consequence of both positive reinforcement and aversion from withdrawal symptoms, a heroin addict is powerfully driven:[42] "he becomes as dependent on drugs as he is on food."[43] The dependence amounts to a grave and permanent limitation of freedom. (Thus, paradoxically, those who, in the name of liberty, claim that everyone should be free to use any drugs he wants endanger potential users with a loss of freedom much more severe than that due to prohibition.)

Prolonged addiction to opiates results in considerable personality change. Since their use becomes the main adjustive mechanism of the addict, desire for them tends to replace all other drives, many of which are useful.[44] The drug addict "becomes lethargic, slovenly, undependable, and devoid of ambition. . . . He loses all desire for socially productive work and exhibits little interest in food, sex, companionship, family ties, or recreation."[45] The addicted adolescent avoids learning new skills to overcome difficulties. Again, a shot of heroin provides an easy and gratifying escape from any problems.[46] The adjustive value of opiates explains clearly why their easy availability would lead a high proportion of maladjusted people to drug use. In times of grave social difficulties, when the number of maladjusted persons grows, the habit "would be acquired by a large segment of the population; and as shown by historical experience in China and Egypt would be a major contributing factor toward perpetuating poverty, ignorance, and lack of social and economic progress."[47]

There are many other unfortunate consequences of opiate addiction. Declining interest in the family results in neglect of the spouse and children. Following a decline in sexual interest, men become impotent, and women cease to menstruate; if, however, an addicted woman becomes pregnant, her unborn child will be physically dependent, and its withdrawal symptoms, which begin hours after birth, may be fatal.[48] Insensitivity to pain makes the addict neglect the signals of disease, and insensitivity to danger makes him neglect the need of escaping from injury.[49] Use of unsterilized needles is responsible for the spread of dangerous infections,[50] and since the range between the rewarding and the lethal dose of opiates is narrow, overdose is a frequent cause of death.

Thus, drug abuse is harmful for both the user and the society. Because of the social harms, prohibition and punishment are feasible from a utilitarian standpoint. Harm for the user is serious enough to make paternalistic prohibition and punishment reasonable. In spite of this, punishment of drug abuse in America amounts to a grave injustice but for reasons very different from those that account for injustice of the norms on homosexual behavior.

There is one basic prerequisite of justice that is commonly accepted not only in America but also in all civilized societies: that there be no crime without guilt. This means that the bare act of breaking criminal law should not be enough to constitute a crime:

40

a subjective element is also needed. It consists in the possibility of blaming the actor for the lawbreaking. The possibility is there if the lawbreaking was intentional, reckless, or, at least, negligent. It is not if the lawbreaking was an outcome of circumstances beyond the actor's control.[51]

Many such circumstances may occur, and one is of particular importance here—the lawbreaker's state of mind. The lawbreaker may be unable to control his behavior, because of infancy, mental deficiency or disease, or a temporary impairment of mental activity. It may consist in the lawbreaker's not understanding what he is doing or in his acting under an irresistible drive that does "destroy the power . . . to choose" not to violate·the law[52]—a drive he has no capacity to overcome. In neither case may he be blamed for what he is doing; he is not guilty, and punishing him would offend the general feeling of justice. "Our collective conscience does not allow punishment where it cannot impose blame," in the well-known words of Judge Arnold.[53]

There are two kinds of drug abuse: by the addicts and by nonaddicted experimenters and beginners. The injustice I am speaking of concerns the former. In the light of the preceding comments the force of addiction should be clear: it is an overwhelming dependence. In particular the drive for heroin is too strong to be overcome by the usual power of will. However miserable the addict's life may be, and however much he may want to rid himself of the habit, he is usually unable to do so. Thus, he should not be blamed for the drug use, and his punishment, like any punishment of innocent behavior, is clearly unjust.[54]

There is more to it, however. By bringing harmful side-effects, the punishment is unwise. It sanctions a prohibition—the addict may not acquire the drug lawfully. Consequently, owing to the power of his drive, he is pushed into its illegal acquisition. This happened for the first time under the Harrison Act, and in its wake, because of the elimination of legitimate sources of supply, a huge narcotics racket started operating. It persists, with all its corrupting influence. Although the costs of producing heroin, if the

41

production is not illicit, are negligible, the price of the racket-provided drug is exorbitant. The average daily cost of supporting a heroin habit amounts, according to a carefully reasoned estimate, to $28 in 1970 prices.[55] The expense exceeds the financial abilities of the majority of addicts, even more so since heroin addiction is associated with poverty—maladjusted and poor people have a more than average chance of becoming addicted,[56] and addiction itself tends to bring increasing poverty. That is why the addict is being pushed into crime just to support his habit. He resorts to theft, burglary, prostitution, drug peddling, and, in particular, robbing and mugging.[57] The amount of property crimes he has to commit is increased by the prevailing five-to-one fencing ratio. To acquire $28 a day, he must take $140 worth of property, which amounts to $50,000 a year. Dividing this "revenue" by the value of an average property crime yields an estimate of twelve crimes per month in a lower income community or six crimes per month in wealthier neighborhoods.[58] The annual cost of heroin-related acquisitive property crime has been estimated at $500 million in New York City and at $2.5 billion in New York State.[59] The estimated annual cost of law enforcement dealing with the acquisitive crime—including investigations, arrests, trials, imprisonment—amounted, in 1974, to $719 million at the federal level only.[60] The frequency of the crime results in "the community's sense of alarm and outrage,"[61] with all its psychological and social consequences.

None of these criminal activities are produced by the pharmacological characteristics of heroin; unlike alcohol, which gives rise to aggressiveness and frequent brutality, the opiates inhibit aggressive impulses.[62] The activities are predominantly caused by the impact of the prohibitive provisions in force. This does not mean that without those provisions all the heroin addicts would have been law-abiding citizens. There is abundant evidence that an unusually high proportion of them commit crimes or delinquent acts prior to the addiction.[63] This is understandable: socially maladjusted persons are particularly addiction prone, and social maladjustment is criminogenic as well. Once heroin dependence does emerge, however, a new and powerful criminogenic factor starts operating: the prohibitive norms of criminal law, which push the addict into acquisitive crime.

All this does not mean that the prohibition should be completely removed, and unlimited distribution of heroin be allowed. The harms of addiction make it necessary to prevent its spread, and criminal law should be used as a preventive implement, on which I shall elaborate later.[64] What I am criticizing here is a totally and blindly imposed ban, as well as punishment of addicts for use of the drug. The punishment is a conspicuous instance of an unjust sanction. It either runs against the dominant feeling of justice or will do so as soon as it becomes generally understood that punishment of the addict amounts to punishment of the innocent.[65]

As in the case of homosexuals the injustice of the punishment brings two further consequences. First, it makes the punishment unpersuasive and thus void of the educative influence. Again, there is nothing troublesome about this; it is not the law's business to persuade the society that an innocent behavior is morally wrong. The second consequence is, however, harmful: the unjust sanctions diminish the society's belief in justice of the lawmakers and courts and thus undermine the general educative power of criminal law. (Furthermore, the ban itself—irrespective of the punishment that sanctions it—can also be perceived as unjust; the morality of a prohibition that brings on the addict all the miseries here described may be challenged. The ban constitutes, however, first of all, an example of unwise law. Its makers have not only failed to prevent behavior they wanted to eliminate but also brought about a number of disastrous consequences. Nevertheless, this is an issue whose analysis exceeds the limits of the present chapter. I am dealing here with the injustice of punishment, not with policy errors of lawmakers.)

CRIMINAL PUNISHMENT

Inconsistency: Judicial Sentencing Powers and Indeterminate Sentences

Sweeping and barely checked discretionary sentencing powers given to judges (and, in a few jurisdictions, to juries) result in an inconsistency that has been called a "tragic state of disorder."[66] Some degree of judicial discretion constitutes, in civilized societies, an important prerequisite of justice. It enables the judge to impose punishment that fits not only the harmfulness of the behavior punished but also the amount of guilt, that is, the amount of moral blame,[67] which may depend, in particular, upon the criminal's personality, his past, and circumstances under which the crime had been committed. But the amount of discretion exercised by the American judge goes far beyond this reason. It has been given to him, under the influence of positivist criminology, as an implement for treatment; the judge should apply punishments that will rehabilitate the criminal.

Two beliefs underlie this notion: first, belief in the general feasibility of rehabilitation and, second, belief in the judge's ability to predict future behavior of the criminal, in particular to predict what kind and amount of punishment will reeducate him. The kind and amount differ from one criminal to another. Thus, in three similar cases of murder, the proper sentence may be 25 years for one murderer, 5 years for the other, and simply probation (or even discharge) for the third, if the third does not constitute risks for the future. Under the impact of this philosophy a judge in Florida may impose, for kidnapping or first degree burglary, any sentence between a fine and imprisonment for life.[68] In Colorado he may impose, for voluntary manslaughter or robbery, a fine or any amount of imprisonment, between one day and ten years.[69] The federal law authorizes punishment by "death, or imprisonment for any term of years or for life" for a rape committed within the special maritime and territorial jurisdiction of the United States.[70]

The general philosophy of reeducating criminals as the pri-

44

mary goal of criminal justice is wrong: it undermines certainty of punishment and makes the lawbreaker, and not the general public, the main addressee of criminal sanctions—a fallacy on which I shall elaborate later.[71] More importantly for the present considerations, the philosophy imposes an impossible burden on the judges: they are supposed to make an accurate prognosis about the impact of differential severity of punishment on the lawbreaker's reeducation. True, sometimes just common sense may make the prognosis feasible; a Manson makes an exceptionally poor bet for reeducation, whereas an act of a genuine mercy killing may make reeducation needless. Our knowledge of human behavior is, however, too limited for safe predictions on the majority of criminals: even professionals—psychologists, psychiatrists, social workers— are unable to make them, and judges are more so. This is why the reeducative effectiveness of punishment could not provide a clear and uniform criterion for determination of its severity; if the legislators make effectiveness the major criterion, they select an extremely vague standard that cannot but turn the sentencing process into a display of arbitrary power.

This is exactly what has happened to much of the sentencing process in the United States. The sweeping penalty statutes make sanctions dependent on the philosophical inclinations, ''character, bias, neurosis, and daily vagary'' encountered among individual judges.[72] On top of that, the judges are not required to give reasons for the sentence, and, under the majority of state jurisdictions, there is no appellate review of sentencing. Thus, when determining the punishment, they may limit themselves to brief, unstructured hunches. ''The judge is likely to read thick briefs, hear oral argument, and then take days or weeks to decide who breached a contract for delivery of onions. The same judge will read a presentence report, perhaps talk to a probation officer, hear a few minutes of pleas for mercy—invest, in sum, less than an hour in all—before imposing a sentence of ten years in prison.'' [73]

There is a peculiar paradox in this. Up to the moment of sentencing, the constitutionally imposed checks against convicting

45

the innocent, and against any abuse of power, pervade the course of the criminal trial. So do the requirements of procedural fairness and of equality before the law. The sentencing is a crucial element of the process. However, when the moment of sentencing arrives, all the checks and requirements suddenly disappear. The sentencing is often of even greater consequence for the defendant than establishment of his innocence or guilt. The difference between having been found guilty or having been acquitted may amount to going on probation or going free. The difference due to the sentencing may amount to going on probation or being imprisoned for life. Still, all the components of the process that influence determination of guilt or innocence are subject to most stringent checks, whereas the sentencing constitutes an act of arbitrary will, unaccounted for, and, at best, supported by a presentence report, where hearsay evidence is often used to discover relevant facts.[74]

The resulting injustices are grave, and they constitute

a pervasive problem in almost all jurisdictions. In the Federal system, for example, the average length of prison sentences for narcotics violations in 1965 was 83 months in the 10th Circuit, but only 44 months in the 3d Circuit. During 1962 the average sentence for forgery ranged from a high of 68 months in the Northern District of Mississippi to a low of 7 months in the Southern District of Mississippi. . . . Disparity among judges sitting in the same court is illustrated by the findings of a recent study of the Detroit Recorder's Court. Over a 20-month period in which the sample cases were about equally distributed among the 10 judges, 1 judge imposed prison terms upon 75 to 90 percent of the defendants whom he sentenced, while another judge imposed prison sentences in about 35 percent of the cases. One judge consistently imposed prison sentences twice as long as those of the most lenient judge.[75]

What does all this mean in terms of individual cases? A well-known report by a former Director of the Federal Bureau of Prisons provides a number of striking instances:

Take . . . the cases of two men we received last spring. The first man had been convicted of cashing a check for $58.40. He was out of work at the time of his offense . . . and when his wife became ill . . . he needed money for rent, food, and doctor bills. . . . He had no prior criminal record. The other man cashed a check for $35.20. He was also out of work and his wife had left him for another man. His prior record consisted of a drunk charge and a nonsupport charge. Our examination of these two cases indicated no significant differences for sentencing purposes. But they appeared before different judges and the first man received 15 years in prison and the second man 30 days.

In one of our institutions a middle-aged credit union treasurer is serving 117 days for embezzling $24,000 in order to cover his gambling debts. On the other hand, another middle-aged embezzler with a fine past record and a fine family is serving 20 years, with 5 years probation to follow. At the same institution is a middle-aged tax accountant who on tax fraud charges received 31 years and 31 days in consecutive sentences [whereas] . . . last year an unstable young man served out his 98-day sentence for armed bank robbery.[76]

However striking these injustices, the philosophy of treatment is responsible for much more than that. Once reeducation becomes the main purpose of criminal sanctions, imprisonment should end exactly at the moment when the inmate gets reeducated. The moment cannot be accurately foreseen in advance. Some argue (and there is merit in the argument) that it may come at any time, after a few months or many years, or never. Consequently, judges should not fix sentences in advance. The period of imprisonment should always be open, and the correctional authorities, being aware of the inmate's rehabilitative progress, should be given continuous discretionary power to keep him in prison or release him, on parole or unconditionally, which would "put before [him] great incentive to well-doing" and eventually result in "the habit of well-doing."[77] That was why a peculiar institution of the indeterminate sentence emerged: a "prison sentence for which the precise term of confinement is not known on the day of judgment but will be subject . . . to the later decision of a parole board or some comparable agency."[78]

The institution was first introduced, amid high expectations, at the Elmira prison in 1877 and then spread throughout the

47

country. After the turn of the century the majority of the states, as well as the federal government, adopted some form of indeterminate sentences. The forms have varied. For instance, Michigan and Pennsylvania introduced fixed maximum penalties and flexible minimums to be set by judges, with eligibility for parole, basically, at minimum. At the Patuxent prison in Maryland the administrative authority might have, before the reform of 1977, released the inmate any time or have kept him incarcerated for life; under the federal law the Board of Parole has been allowed, in principle, to grant parole any time between completion of one-third and two-thirds of the judge-imposed sentence. These and other variants won considerable support among legal writers, judges, law enforcement officials;[79] as late as 1968 the draftsmen of the Model Penal Code displayed "full agreement with the proposition that the sentencing structure should be dominated by the principle of indeterminacy."[80]

The resulting injustice is, however, even worse than that due to the sweeping judicial discretion. The administrative agencies are, for the most part, as unable to predict the future behavior of a criminal as the judge is: "If judges are not social scientists . . . , most parole board members are not either and even where some of them are, there is no evidence that their decisions . . . are more wise . . . than those of judges;"[81] often the opposite is true, since they are much more dependent on political pressures and fluctuation of public opinion.[82] They rely on reports of prison personnel, but the qualifications of the personnel are predominantly meager[83] and the reports arbitrary;[84] moreover, many inmates learn how to deceive the personnel—to get out of confinement, they simulate remorse and repentance and attend with sham eagerness therapeutic programs they consider meaningless and silly.[85] The parole boards and similar agencies proceed quickly (before 1976, when California abandoned indeterminate sentences, it took an average of 14 minutes for the Adult Authority in California to question an inmate at an annual hearing)[86], and they reach unreviewable decisions in secret, without explanation.[87] Consequently, the decisions result in gradation of punishments at least as inconsistent as that engendered by the judicial discretion.

Furthermore, the capriciously applied principle of indeterminacy is itself inherently cruel. It means that the inmate never knows when the confinement will end. This results in permanent anxiety and helplessness—a suffering that prisoners call a "constant mental torture of never really knowing how long you'll be here,"[88] and "a perfect hell that drives a person mad."[89] This explains why even inmates with long terms—for whom indeterminacy may be considered as a chance—despise the indeterminate sentence. One only wonders why, until recently, there had been no widespread public outcry against it. Public indifference seems to provide an explanation: "Prisoners are—according to the most remarkable report issued a few years ago—nearly always out of sight and out of mind for the vast majority of people."[90] On the other hand, prison administrators are the least expected to help in arousing anybody's interest; for them indeterminate sentences constitute a convenient management device. Just after their introduction more than 100 years ago the number of cases requiring corporal punishment of inmates declined, according to one warden, by 75 percent, and today many correctional systems in the United States depend on the discretionary power of parole boards to control prisoners:[91] "the slightest infraction, the smallest offense, even the half-joking insult, may . . . be inserted in their records and affect their release dates."[92]

Nevertheless, owing to the activity of various groups and individuals and to the impact of some recent court decisions,[93] the interest in indeterminate sentences is growing and the contempt for them spreading. Its embattled supporters complain that "the indeterminate sentence is under attack nationwide."[94] Following the attack, it has been removed from some state laws in recent years, in particular in California, Illinois, and Maine, and a number of other states are considering its removal; in 1977 the Judiciary Committee of the Senate recommended its abolishment at the federal level.[95] Thus, in the years to come, the indeterminate sentence may become just a sad footnote to the history of American law. Today, however, it persists in federal law and in laws of many states, and since it runs against the steadily spreading moral sentiment, it is becoming an unjust punishment—in the here accepted metaethical meaning of "injustice."

Inconsistency: Plea Bargaining

The system of criminal justice in the United States is overburdened: crime rates are high, and criminal trials are slow, expensive, and demanding. An average full-scale trial takes several days.[96] Its government-borne costs include the time of judges and other court employees, prosecutors, public defenders, experts, jurors, and others. Their time is expensive: salaries of trial judges in state courts range from $25,000 to $49,000,[97] and trial juror costs in federal courts alone amount to nearly $16 million per year.[98] Demanding constitutional standards may make the presentation of incriminating evidence difficult or even impossible owing to the application of exclusionary rule. The criminal court system could effectively handle a very large caseload if the procedure were brief, inexpensive, and flexible, or it could decide a small number of cases in long, expensive, and rigidly structured trials. However, a conjunction of very large numbers and a very demanding procedure is, granted limitation of resources, impossible and must result in some kind of economizing, *praeter legem* or even *contra legem*.

The American system has responded to the conjunction by a peculiar way of economizing: it encourages defendants to plead guilty for leniency. The bargain, negotiated most often between the prosecutor and defendant or his attorney, is simple: the defendant consents to conviction without trial in return for mitigation of his sentence, and the judge imposes the sentence without delay.

The bargaining is not always a prerequisite for a plea of guilty. Some criminals, remorseful for the crime committed, feel they ought to confess (and this feeling seems to match a wide-spread moral sentiment).[99] Some others realize that, in view of their obvious guilt and its convincing evidence, "a trial is not worth the agony and expense" to themselves and their families.[100] These motivations account, however, only for a minor part of the guilty pleas; the overwhelming majority of them are being entered in exchange for leniency. Thus, since about 90 percent of all convictions in the United States are by pleas of guilty,[101] the greatest part of all the convictions are obtained by plea bargaining. The bargaining has become such an "essential component of the administration of justice" that its abrupt decline would result in chaos. "If every criminal charge were subjected to a full-scale trial, the States and the Federal Government would need to multiply by many times the number of judges and court facilities,"[102] of jurors, prosecutors, police officers, and public defenders—an objective that may be impractical in view of limited financial and human resources.

The practice of plea bargaining is not only economically expedient but also rewarding for all the participants in the disposition of criminal cases: judges, prosecutors, and defense attorneys. By avoiding trial, the judge saves time and escapes the risk of being reversed.[103] The prosecutor saves time and "eliminates the risk of defeat."[104] Moreover, plea bargaining secures a conviction, however light, in weak cases, and many prosecutors feel that "half a loaf is better than none." It is evidently better for themselves: conviction statistics are "a tangible measure of their success,"[105] and the more convictions they secure, the higher their chance for reelection or promotion. It also might be perceived as better for the society; if a defendant is guilty, and if proving the charge may be too difficult, it is easy to assume that public interest demands a lenient punishment rather than no punishment at all.[106] The defense attorney, by compromising in plea negotiations and thus making the work of the judge and prosecutor easier, earns their smooth cooperation on which he largely depends.[107] Moreover, the public defender saves time by avoiding trial, whereas for

51

private defense attorneys guilty pleas constitute the easiest way of making money. When accepting the case, many of them collect a single fee to cover all the services through trial, and a plea means that they keep the money and avoid the work. They maintain, however, that their interest in pleading guilty does converge with interests of the defendants: the defendants get leniency[108] and avoid pains of trial and, if the bargain results in charge reduction, the stigma of being convicted for a major crime.[109] Thus, the negotiated pleas provide for a smooth, prompt, and economic operation of the adjudicative process and meet the professional needs of the bureaucratic subculture that handles the process. Consequently, the pleas replace the officially prescribed, formal court procedure. This happens in a manner characteristic of many bureaucratic institutions: bureaucracies tend to satisfy their internal needs—efficiency of operations and interests of officials—at the expense of their stated social functions, and the satisfaction is being facilitated by informal, discretionary manipulations that replace strictly regulated and visible procedures.[110]

As an economic and bureaucratic expediency, plea bargaining emerged long ago. Having been on a steady increase since the early nineteenth century, it reduced convictions by jury to a small fraction of all the convictions as early as in the 1920s.[111] But then it was an "under the table," unrecognized practice. Only in recent years has it become explicitly approved by the judiciary; the bargained stipulation has been acknowledged as basically binding[112] and even respectable; according to Chief Justice Burger, if "[p]roperly administered, it should be encouraged."[113] It would be difficult to agree with this evaluation. However expedient it is, and despite its new judicial approval, law enforcement that relies on plea bargaining becomes, in the words published more than 50 years ago but fully valid today, "a farce and travesty upon justice."[114] True, judges, prosecutors, defense attorneys, and many defendants benefit from it, but the whole society becomes a loser. Indeed, bargained pleas should be perceived as conspiracies to obstruct justice rather than as components of its administration.

JUSTICE

Several descriptive and statistical studies have thrown light on how bargained pleas are arranged. To avoid trial, a plea of guilty is needed; thus, the defendant must be persuaded to confess his guilt. The persuasion comes sometimes from the judge, more often from the prosecutor, and most frequently from the defense counsel.[115] When persuading, the counsel acts, not only as the defendant's adviser, but also in the interests of all those involved in the disposition of the case, especially of the judge and prosecutor, and he impresses the defendant that the judge and the prosecutor would cooperate. The judge and the prosecutor expect the defense counsel to use such persuasion. If he balks, they often press him to do so.[116]

The persuasion consists most frequently in the promise that the prosecutor will recommend a light sentence, reduce the charge, or dismiss some of the multiple charges against the defendant. The higher the impending penalty, the more effective the persuasion; in particular, a defendant accused convincingly of a capital crime will have a strong incentive to plead guilty for reduction of the charge. To provide incentives in less perilous cases, prosecutors use the technique of overcharging—"vertical" and "horizontal." The former means threatening defendants with punishment for the gravest crime conceivable, for example, for first-degree murder in the event of any homicide. The second means threatening a multiplicity of charges and penalties. The threats are used in a variety of circumstances, in particular, if a defendant committed a number of criminal acts, if a continuous crime (like daily embezzlements by an employee) can be construed as an aggregate of separate offenses, if a single act violates several provisions of criminal law (like a forcible incestuous act with a girl of 10), and if a single act results in a number of harms (like a case of arson in which many lives have been lost).[117]

Under scrupulously made criminal codes of some foreign countries there is no room for horizontal overcharging. The codes contain provisions that determine in advance the amount of punishment in the event of aggregation of criminal acts or harms and of

53

the aggregation of penal norms violated by a single act.[118] Such provisions are absent from criminal laws in the United States. The absence leaves the determination of amount of punishment within discretionary powers of the courts; a judge may either make an arbitrary selection of one of the grounds for punishment or add penalties together and sentence the defendant for a long time— sometimes for hundreds of years. That is why horizontal over-charging can be effectively used by the prosecution to induce defendants to plead guilty.

There are many more inducements in use. One of them is the very fact of waiting for trial in jail, especially by the indigent defendant who cannot make bail. Inhuman jail conditions make him more likely to plead guilty the longer he waits. "If he stays in jail for six months or a year, which is not unusual, a judge is likely to sentence him to 'time served' if he pleads guilty to a minor crime [and] . . . [h]e goes home free."[119] If, however, he refuses to cooperate, he will be waiting longer in the jail for trial and risk a subsequent penalty in the event of conviction. Some defense counsels use delaying tactics in order to "soften" the defendant and bring him to a bargain by keeping him longer in jail.[120] The defendant's family and friends are also used. Defense counsels often ask the defendant's spouse or next of kin "to appeal to [him] to 'help himself' by pleading guilty."[121] On the other hand, prosecutors use threats to prosecute his family members and friends unless he makes a plea. For instance, in a leading case—*Kent v. United States*[122]—the defendant was told that his fiancée would be charged as an accessory unless he pleaded guilty, and many other threats of this kind have been reported by courts.[123]

Whenever a judge "becomes a participant in plea bargaining, he brings to bear the full force . . . of his office. His awesome power to impose a substantially longer or even maximum sentence in excess of that proposed . . . [subjects] the accused to a . . . powerful influence,"[124] and the influence is sometimes direct and brutal.[125] True, direct bargaining by judges is rather rare: they expect defense counsels and prosecutors to exercise the

54

pressure. Even without direct participation, however, the air of judicial involvement is there: the defendant understands that the judge cooperates with the defense counsel and the prosecutor and will either repay a guilty plea with leniency or impose a harsh sentence upon conviction after trial. To make this apprehension credible, "an example occasionally must be made of the uncooperative individual who contests the case unsuccessfully."[126] Thus, a severe penalty is used, in the case of recalcitrants, to motivate acquiescence from others.[127]

The Court pretended, until recently, not to have known of the bargained pleas and of the inducements and pressures involved. No wonder. An ideal model of the criminal procedure has been traditionally professed in America, and the Court-led "constitutional revolution" brought its further refinement. The model implies trial by jury as a constitutional right of every defendant. The trial must be held in the open. It protects the innocent by the assumption of innocence and by a requirement of a demanding proof of guilt. It ensures, moreover, both the protection of the innocent and suitable punishment of the guilty by proper presentation of evidence and by its severe testing in an adversary manner. It also ensures a great amount of fairness to all defendants, innocent and guilty alike. Consequently, the evidence against the defendant must be obtained by fair means if it is to be used at trial. This holds, in particular, with respect to confessions as an evidence of guilt. The privilege against self-incrimination, always cherished in America, became, in the 1960s, extended by the Court to federal and state-run custodial interrogation and was construed very broadly: any pressure to confess, however mild, amounts to infringement of fairness and thus of the privilege. Even minor and unintentional deprivations inherent in any interrogation have been held unfair and, if confession was obtained, resulted in reversal of convictions. To prevent the use of any influence, and thus to inhibit all confessions except those entirely free and voluntary, the Court introduced the *Miranda* warnings in 1966.

Thus, a criminal trial in the United States is governed by

very high standards. However, only about 5 percent of all criminal cases go to trial by jury, whereas approximately 90 percent are being settled by a negotiated plea; and when plea bargaining starts, all the lofty ideals are gone. First of all, the defendant's constitutional right to trial is infringed once he is advised to plead guilty; the suggestion implies a heavy penalty for the exercise of the right. Gone is the openness of the procedure; negotiated cases are disposed in a confidential and discretionary way, hardly accessible to judicial or public scrutiny, and this practice brings danger of abuse, especially on the part of prosecutors and defense counsels.[128]

Gone also is the ideal of adversary struggle to test the accusation; a mixture of bartering and bureaucratic cooperation replaces the combat. The bartering resembles a gamble; since the prosecutor and the defense counsel are not certain of the facts of the case they negotiate or of each other's knowledge of the facts, they often resort to bluffing.[129] The cooperation results in dangerous conflicts of roles and interests on the part of those involved in the bargaining process. The prosecutor is supposed to prosecute in care of the public interest, and the defense counsel, to defend assiduously. However, when negotiating a plea, both of them perform a sentencing role;[130] if the negotiation results in an arbitrary reduction of the charge, they assume, by nullifying prescribed penalties, the role of lawmakers. The judge is supposed to apply the law in force, but, when knowingly accepting a reduced charge as ground for conviction, he also assumes a legislative function: he creates an offense "out of thin air, and someone is punished for it. Another offense is actually committed and no one is punished."[131] He should apply the law as an impartial arbiter—a role difficult to reconcile with coercing guilty pleas. The conflict of interests is most marked on the part of the defense counsel. His client is entitled to a vigorous defense, whereas he develops a professional and financial interest in a smooth and speedy negotiation of the case. Consequently, he is often tempted to disregard the defendant's interest. This is particularly true of a public defender. If vigorous defense of a case endangers his working relationship with the prosecutor or the judge, he may feel compelled to trade-out an occasional triable case, and, by delivering a guilty plea, to ensure favorable treatment of his many other cases and to promote his future career.[132]

Finally, two other basic elements of the ideal procedural model become victims of plea bargaining. The first is the assumption of innocence; pressing the defendant to plead guilty without careful scrutiny of evidence amounts to assumption of guilt on his part (which means an increased risk of convicting the innocent). Second, gone is the high standard of fairness set by the Court's extensive reading of the privilege against self-incrimination. Thus, on the whole, there seems to be some hypocrisy in the fact that all the great and proudly pronounced constitutional ideals, while influential at the relatively few tried cases, are absent from the vast majority of criminal dispositions.

All this means that, from the viewpoint of its own standards, the Court should have struck out plea bargaining as an unconstitutional practice. However, unless combined with a restructuring of the whole system of criminal justice, this would have resulted in a breakdown of the system. Since the restructuring was out of the reach of the judicial branch, the Court understandably preferred not to have known of the practice and, until quite recently, avoided considering its validity. This reluctant stand has changed, however, and, in 1969 and 1970, certiorari was granted in a number of cases challenging plea negotiations.

Plea bargaining survived the challenge and emerged as a legitimate practice. The Court acknowledged it as ''an essential part of the criminal process.''[133] Negotiated ''guilty pleas are not constitutionally forbidden, because . . . we cannot hold,'' claimed Justice White for the majority in *Brady v. United States*[134] ''that it is unconstitutional for the State to extend a benefit to a defendant who in turn extends a substantial benefit to the State and who demonstrates by his plea that he is ready and willing to admit his crime.''

CRIMINAL PUNISHMENT

Having acknowledged the negotiated pleas, the Court faced a difficult dilemma. Traditionally, a guilty plea, to be valid, had to be voluntary,[135] that is, to meet the "voluntariness-totality of circumstances" test—a high standard of fairness (however, less demanding than the Warren Court requirements for confessions). Did the acknowledgement of plea bargaining amount to abandonment of the voluntariness requirement or to accepting its new meaning? The Court selected the latter option and drew a new demarcation line between voluntary and coerced guilty pleas. To be voluntary, a plea has to fulfill two conditions. First, the defendant must make it intelligently, with an awareness of its consequences, especially of "the advantages and disadvantages of a trial as compared with those attending a plea of guilty;"[136] and the awareness depends heavily on presence of defense counsel.[137] Second, it has to be made without threats or promises other than those intrinsic in a plea agreement—in particular without "actual or threatened physical harm," promises "having no proper relationship to the prosecutor's business," and without misrepresentation, that is, "unfulfilled or unfulfillable promises."[138]

According to this demarcation line, a guilty plea was held involuntary, and thus set aside, when there were doubts "whether the defendant understood the nature of the charge" to which he pleaded guilty,[139] when a trial judge accepting a plea did not employ "the utmost solicitude" to make sure the defendant had "a full understanding to what the plea connotes and of its consequence,"[140] and when a prosecutor (or a judge) who promised leniency failed to adhere to the promise.[141] On the other hand, the Court did not consider involuntary a plea of guilty "motivated by a coerced confession unless the defendant was incompetently advised by his attorney"[142] and, more importantly, a plea "entered to avoid the possibility of a death penalty,"[143] even if the defendant "took the stand and testified that he had not committed the [crime] but that he was pleading guilty because he faced the threat of the death penalty if he did not do so."[144] Thus, in the name of expediency, the meaning of "voluntariness" has been stretched by

58

the Court beyond its limits set by the legal tradition and by common language.

However deplorable all these outcomes of plea bargaining are, one of its effects is most unfortunate: plea bargaining makes criminal punishment completely inconsistent. Were it not for the bargaining, the court could rather impose, in each case, a penalty prescribed by the norm of criminal law that sanctions the offense committed; and if the norm provides discretionary boundaries, the measure of punishment might be fixed, ideally, in consonance with the amount of guilt. Thus, the penalties would be distributed according to fairly uniform criteria. Under plea bargaining, lightening the sentence within discretionary boundaries does not result from insignificance of guilt or any other uniform principle but depends on how all the participants have played the negotiating game. Dismissal of some of the multiple charges is equally arbitrary. Reduction of charge means application of an arbitrarily selected criminal norm that has not been broken at all. The arbitrariness results in inconsistency; the negotiated penalties differ, in like cases, from case to case, judge to judge, and court to court. The basic requirement of justice—treat like cases alike—is gone, and thus gone is the just character of criminal dispositions.

Two extremes of the arbitrariness are particularly striking (and neither can be easily avoided despite the new trend toward making plea bargaining more open and structured). The first consists in convicting innocent defendants. Plea bargaining increases the risk of their conviction, and the convictions seem occasionally to occur;[145] this amounts not only to injustice by treating like cases differently but also to injustice in "absolute" terms. The other, very frequent extreme consists in letting the criminal go free, on probation or otherwise, without any rationale except expediency; this means an infringement not only of justice but also of certainty of punishment—an issue to which I shall return.

However haphazard the negotiated penalties are, they are subject to some regularities that make them even more unjust. First, there is a more-than-chance probability that a negotiated penalty will be harsher than average if the defendant is guilt ridden, or ignorant, or poor. There are several reasons for this. One of them is that, owing to his feeling of guilt, an occasional defendant may plead guilty without considering any negotiations. An ignorant defendant may not know about the possibility of bargaining or misunderstand how the bargaining process operates.[146] If the defendant is too poor to make bail, he may be kept in pretrial detention, which greatly diminishes his bargaining power. Moreover, he may be unable to hire a private attorney, and public defenders are handicapped in the pursuit of some bargaining strategies, for example, delaying tactics or judge shopping.[147]

On the other hand, there is a more-than-chance probability that the worst offenders will be rewarded by the most excessive leniency: a "professional and habitual criminal . . . generally [has] expert legal advice and [is] best able to take full advantage of the bargaining opportunity."[148] He not only uses every available procedural device but also feigns "an appropriate . . . degree of guilt, penitence and remorse," to make his hearers believe "that he is contrite and thereby merits a lesser plea."[149] Moreover, he often uses informing as an important bargaining chip, especially informing on his accomplices. This information, and possible testimony, are useful to law enforcement. Thus, if he is motivated by remorse and by an acceptance of responsibility, it is meritorious of him to painfully break the loyalty to his friends for the greater social good. However, the information provided by him is self-serving. The repentance is not there, the loyalty to the society has not been restored, and, whatever loyalties he has had to his friends and accomplices he breaks to make a better bargain for himself.[150] Thus, the more shrewd and ruthless a criminal is, the better he is served by the administration of the "negotiated justice."

The unjust (and constitutionally dubious) character of the "negotiated justice" may be perceived as wrong per se, irrespective of its harmful consequences. However, from the standpoint of this study one of its consequences is most important: its destructive impact on the educative power of criminal punishment—indeed, it is much more destructive than punishing homosexual behavior or drug abuse.

The prerequisites of the educative power have been deduced, in the first chapter of this book, from the general account of persuasive instrumental learning: to use punishment as an effective implement of moral learning, the punishing agent must make of it a persuasive moral communication. Thus, he must impress the punished subject and observers that the punishment is being applied because the punished behavior was intrinsically wrong, and to do so, he must impose a just punishment. Moreover, he himself must be respected and trusted: his prestige enhances the persuasiveness.

Do judges, by imposing negotiated penalties, tell anyone that defendants are being punished for wrongdoing? They convict "[a]rmed robbers . . . of attempted assault in the third degree; car thieves with unauthorized entry into a motor vehicle; child molesters with loitering in a school yard."[151] The judicial decision seems to convey to the defendant a mean message: you are being rewarded for yielding your constitutional rights, for having a shrewd lawyer, for your ruthlessness and ability to take advantage from the sale of sentences for pleas; or you are being penalized for not being cooperative enough, for being too poor to hire a good lawyer, for being too decent or too naive to bargain ruthlessly and make the best deal possible. Thus, it is at least dubious whether negotiated punishments sound as moral communications at all; even if they do, their unjust character makes them void of persuasive moral influence. That is why they are much more harmful than the wrong selection of behavior to be punished. If punishment of homosexuals or drug addicts does not persuade the society that homosexual acts among consenting adults in private or drug use by those addicted are immoral, nothing troublesome happens; behavior of the former is harmless, and that of the latter, innocent. Plea bargaining, on the other hand, destroys the moral persuasiveness of punishments imposed for all kinds of genuine wrongdoing.

CRIMINAL PUNISHMENT

Moreover, negotiated punishments ruin the prestige of the courts and judges (and in this they resemble the wrong selection of behavior to be punished). The defendants, as well as the general public, learn how courts nullify the duly constituted law, how judges abandon the role of impartial arbiters, and how intimidation is used to ensure a surrender of constitutional rights. They learn how unjust the resulting court decisions are. They also discover the hypocrisy of the fact that the highest standards of justice and fairness govern the trial but are absent from 90 percent of criminal dispositions. All this undermines trust in and respect for criminal courts and judges and contributes to the annihilation of persuasive moral power of the penalties they impose.

Chapter Three

CERTAINTY

PERFECT CERTAINTY OF punishment means that every crime is punished. This is an ideal that cannot be fully achieved even under a most rigorously arranged legal system and even if criminal punishment were limited to serious wrongdoing. It is impossible to apprehend and convict every criminal without a general abolishment of basic rights and liberties, and their abolishment would result in a new (and much worse) uncertainty. Common criminals would be, in a way characteristic of totalitarian systems, replaced by criminals in government, and punishment of those latter would become not only uncertain but barely possible at all. That is why the ideal of perfect certainty is utopian. A close approximation to it can, however, be achieved without political danger, and, for reasons outlined in the first part of this book, its achievement is essential.

It is not being achieved in the United States at all. Criminal punishment not only is intermittent but also constitutes a very rare response to crime. According to the estimate emerging from 1975 statistics,[1] 20 percent of the total amount of the crimes reported by the FBI[2] result in arrest of a suspect (however, the more severe the crime, the higher the arrest rate), 18 percent result in charge, and 6 percent, in conviction. Well over one-half of convicted criminals immediately go on probation, and thus the proportion of the crimes punished shrinks to less than 3 percent of those known. Moreover, since a substantial part of criminal behavior, especially of minor offenses, goes unnoticed by the police,[3] (with disbelief in effectiveness of law enforcement as the most important reason for nonreporting by the victims[4]), the crimes punished constitute an even smaller fraction of all crimes committed. Thus, "the proportion of actual offenses that result in prison sentences is . . . commonly estimated as being 1 percent of the total number of actual crimes committed, although it varies from crime to crime."[5]

Several factors explain the failure to enforce criminal law. Some of them are commonplace or of limited importance, for example, an occasional imperfection of police investigative tactics, an inadequacy of a police force, or various deficiencies in treatment of the witnesses by courts. Two factors are, however, of crucial importance. The first is leniency. It results from the discretionary power on the part of the police, prosecutors, and judges. They are largely free to apprehend, prosecute, convict, and imprison the criminal or to let him go unpunished; more often than not, they let him go. When doing so, they act, to a high degree, under the impact of an elaborate ideology—a peculiar set of sociological and psychological notions. The second factor consists in constitutional constraints on obtaining evidence. I shall discuss the leniency and its underlying ideology first and then the constitutional limitations.

The Leniency

In the legal tradition of this country, punishing criminals has never been perceived as a process to be systematically enforced. From

64

the American Revolution through much of the nineteenth century, criminal sanctions of the state laws were loosely applied. Not only were police and prosecutor staffs weak, but, in addition, the juries "had right to do as they pleased,"[6] the judges were, under the guise of construction, maximizing their discretion, and governors exercised their pardoning power profusely—a stand at least partially explainable by the extreme severity of many sanctions and the triviality of many offenses.[7] Thus, in the formative period of the American legal system, there did not emerge, on the part of those who administered criminal justice, a legal obligation to enforce penalties rigorously, nor did it emerge later. This means, in particular, that today, at least as far as the law in action is concerned, the police are not duty bound to arrest every apprehensible criminal;[8] the prosecution, to prosecute every triable crime; the court, to convict every criminal provable or even proved guilty; and those who administer penalties, to implement every punishment imposed. On each of these levels the law enforcement is discretionary, and the discretion is exercised largely in an arbitrary manner.

The discretion starts with the police. As already noted, according to the law on the books, it is the duty of the police to systematically apprehend known criminals. However, the police have traditionally arrested them only selectively. The lawmakers, aware of the selectiveness, respond by overshooting: they cover by criminal prohibitions an excessively broad range of behavior and expect the police to strike the balance by intermittent enforcement. This makes systematic enforcement not only even more difficult but also unwarranted as well.[9] The arrests are, however, selective mainly with respect to offenses considered as less serious, such as larceny, drunkeness, vagrancy, gambling, drug abuse, traffic violations, and sexual crimes. When a crime perceived by the community as dangerous is being committed, public pressure on the police to enforce the law increases, and the selectivity tends to disappear—having encountered a murderer, the police are not free to let him go. Moreover, since "most serious crime is committed by repeaters, most [dangerous] criminals eventually get arrested.''[10] That is why, from the standpoint of punitive certainty, the police discretion is less harmful than the arbitrary powers given prosecutors and judges.

Their powers are sweeping. First, prosecuting attorneys may dismiss triable cases. They may do so only within constraints imposed by public opinion and other political pressures, but the constraints work imperfectly; in particular, occupational and corporate crimes go most often unindicted, for want of well-organized public resentment.[11] Public resentment against violent, especially predatory, crime is much stronger, and understandably so: ''To steal, to rape, to rob, to assault—these acts are destructive of the very possibility of society and affronts to the humanity of their victims.''[12] That is why prosecutors rarely respond to them by dismissal. However, they often offer a lenient recommendation, with a frequent reduction of charge, in exchange for a plea of guilty, and judges impose lenient sentences in fulfillment of the bargain. Furthermore, the judges are free to grant leniency *sua sponte,* regardless of any bargaining at all.

The leniency most often amounts to a complete or almost complete abandonment of punishment. In the most frequent case the judge suspends, after a plea or verdict of guilty, either the pronouncement of a sentence or the execution of a sentence already pronounced and lets the defendant go on probation. As shown by a scrupulous inquiry, 53 percent of all the offenders sentenced to confinement in 1965—684,000 of 1,282,000—were placed on probation.[13] Since then an even broader use of probation has been widely recommended[14] and adopted; according to a projection it increased to 58 percent in 1975,[15] and is even higher in various crime-ridden regions. For instance, in 1969, only 23 percent of felons, predominantly dealers, convicted on narcotics charges in New York State went to prison,[16] as did, in 1970, only 27 percent of the robbers with a major prior record convicted in Los Angeles County.[17] Thus, if the displeasure of going through the proceedings or of being on probation—a rather minor nuisance, especially when compared with a major crime—is disregarded, not only the overwhelming majority of all criminals, but even the majority of convicted criminals go unpunished.

Discretion and leniency responsible for the intermittence of criminal punishment are expedient. They unburden the overworked police. They are, for the most part, an outcome of plea bargaining, and plea bargaining alleviates overburdening of the court system. They bring relief to the increasingly overcrowded prisons. The expediency is simple: if the police force faces too many suspects, it is convenient not to apprehend them; if those apprehended are too numerous to be tried by courts, it is convenient not to try them; and if too many have been convicted to accommodate them in prison, it is convenient to let them go.

There is much more than that, however, behind the widespread nonenforcement of criminal law in America—indeed, pure expediency of this kind would hardly be tolerable in a democratic society. An elaborate and influential system of antipunitive ideology has developed in this country that makes nonpunishment of criminals not just expedient but worthy. The system consists of two components, sociological and psychological. The former concentrates on crime causation, especially on social determinants of criminal behavior rather than on responsibility of individual offenders. The latter considers treatment and rehabilitation of criminals, rather than punishment, as the main objective of sound policy. Both of them are fallacious: their logic is dubious, and their practical implications are destructive.

Sociological Fallacy: Social Determinants of Criminal Behavior

The most comprehensive attack against consistent and certain application of criminal penalties was launched as a reaction to the classical school of criminology. The founders of the school, especially Beccaria, had assumed a rational and hedonistic calculus of pleasure and pain as the basic human motivation. They believed that anticipation of an inevitable punishment would effectively deter potential lawbreakers and recommended that punishment be inevitable (and uniform and of reasonable severity). The recommendations influenced, since the late 1700s, criminal laws and practices all over Europe and apparently contributed, during the subsequent century, to improvement of crime control in various European countries.

The attack against the classical school came from divergent directions. Many of the adversaries, influenced by positivist philosophy, considered Beccaria's notions of free will and rational choice as metaphysical speculation. They opted for criminology as a natural science discovering general laws and looking for causal explanation of criminal behavior. The first among them—adherents of the positive school founded by Lombroso—claimed the existence of innate, organic characteristics of the criminal that inevitably produce crime.[18] The claim was refuted, however.[19]

Subsequently two other schools have become much more influential, in particular in the United States. One of them, the psychiatric, especially the psychoanalytical, perceives the criminal as driven by unconscious, basically irresistible powers of his mind—and I shall return to this perspective later. The second, on which I shall comment now, stresses environmental and, in particular, social determinants of criminal behavior: this is the intellectual tradition that, having originated from the works of Tarde, Durkheim, and Marx, is being continued in this country by the most numerous groups of crime causation theorists. All of them consider search for causes as "the scientific" approach, contrasting with Beccaria's speculation. They perceive the search as more than just an intellectual exercise, however: once we know the social conditions that generate crime, we can remove them and thus prevent criminal behavior. Ideally, one or a few precisely defined conditions for any crime (or for the majority of crimes) should be discovered. This would provide an optimal basis for policies: once known, one or the few conditions could be easily eliminated and crime prevented.

In their search the American criminologists have identified a large number of social determinants of criminal behavior. One important school stresses, in a variety of ways, bad companions—association with criminals, especially in youth peer groups.[20] Numerous writers stress deficient upbringing, in particular, difficult childhood in broken families.[21] Others add density of population and impersonal relations in urban areas, high mobility, social change, cultural conflicts, emergence of large cohorts of young people following periods of high birth rate, declining role of religion, and so forth. Still others stress economic inequality and poverty—frustrations of being deprived, unemployed, or of living in a slum. An influential school treats inequality, within a broader framework of the anomie theory, as a cause of many crimes: Americans are taught to compete for wealth and status, but economic inequality deprives many of lawful access to either; therefore, to achieve wealth and status, some of the deprived reject legal norms and resort to crime.[22] The Marxists go further in pursuit of generality of the economic explanation: they consider private investment property and the resulting class structure of the society as the determinant of all criminal behavior.

There is a strong determinist component in many of these notions: their inventors consider criminal behavior to be produced unavoidably, or almost unavoidably, by the social forces beyond the criminal's control. (Positivists and many psychoanalysts also opt for a determinist stand: the respective biological or mental influences operating in some men inevitably make criminals of them.) Thus, on the part of someone who has been exposed to their impact, the forces leave little or no room for the use of will to avoid commitment of crime. In this manner the metaphysics of the entirely free will of the classical school has been replaced by the metaphysics of extreme social determinism (or biological or "mental" determinism).

The implications of the replacement are obvious. If the criminal, ridden by forces he is unable to control, has no choice, ascribing guilt to him is nonsense, and punishing him is both morally wrong and purposeless. How can anybody be punished for having bad parents, being born in poverty, growing up in the slum, or being, since early childhood, discriminated against? The more so that all these and many other criminogenic influences have been brought about by the general society, that is by all of us; we are at fault rather than the criminal whom we produced. How, then, can we, the guilty society, punish him, the innocent victim of our institutions? The only humane and reasonable policy would be to abandon sanctioning crime and to remove the root causes, in particular, all the social ills that generate crime—poverty, economic inequality, racial discrimination, family irresponsibility, and others.

The impact of this ideology in the United States is astounding. It may have something to do with the widespread complex of guilt—for the plight of the blacks, the Indians, the poor. The ideology is being proclaimed by a variety of journalists, clergymen, politicians and policy makers, sociologists and social philosophers, and this is just a sample of the proclamations. The "ills within our ghettos, the burdens of our socially and economically deprived and our system's inability to deal with the underlying problems . . . cause most criminality." [23] If thus "a criminal does what he must do . . . it is obviously both futile and unjust to punish him as if he could go straight and had deliberately chosen to do otherwise." [24] "The only way in the world to abolish crime and criminals is to . . . [m]ake fair conditions of life. Give men a chance to live. Abolish the right of private ownership of land, abolish monopoly, make the world partners in production, partners in the good things of life. . . . There should be no jails." [25] "We need, above all, to give far more attention to prevention of crime by attacking its causes and breeding grounds through an intensified battle to eliminate poverty, unemployment, inadequate housing, inferior education. . . . What we need is to build a good society [and] . . . to move away from the punishment ideology and objective." [26]

This philosophy, "widespread among the most influential and articulate contemporary leaders of public opinion," [27] has considerable impact on the legal profession. The President's Commission on Law Enforcement and Administration of Justice claims that "unless society does take concerted action to change the general conditions and attitudes that are associated with crime, no improvement in law enforcement and administration of justice . . . will be of much avail," [28] and this means an "action designed to eliminate slums and ghettos, to improve education, to provide jobs, to make sure that every American is given the opportunities and the freedoms that will enable him to assume his responsibilities. We will not have dealt effectively. with crime until we have alleviated the conditions that stimulate it." [29] In the words of a former Attorney General of the United States, "[i]f we are to control crime, we must undertake a massive effort to rebuild our cities and ourselves, to improve the human condition, to educate, employ, house and make healthy." [30] In this atmosphere it is feasible for some judges (and prosecutors, defense attorneys, and other participants in the criminal process) to assume "that the institution of prison probably must end" [31] and, for many more, to find the practice of intermittent enforcement of criminal law not only expedient, but also legitimate and respectable.

This ideological support of poor law enforcement is unfortunate. To be sure—and the point could hardly be overstated—efforts to solve broad social problems and the suffering they bring are worthwhile for obvious reasons and irrespective of whether the suffering generates criminal behavior. But an attempt to control crime exclusively or mainly by solving the problems is hopeless.

First, the degree to which persistence of criminal behavior depends on each of the problems is unclear. In any society (and the more so if the analysis exceeds narrow spatiotemporal limitations) the term *crime* denotes many kinds of very different behavior. Owing to this heterogeneity, the number of social determinants of criminal behavior is almost unlimited, even at a close level of the causal distance, and it grows while we draw back along the causal paths. That is why the social problems listed here constitute but a small fraction of the many determinants, and it is dubious whether solving them would prevent all or even the majority of crimes.[32] The Marxist fallacy is a case in point here. If Marxist belief in private investment property as a necessary condition for all crimes had been true, the removal of the property would have brought about a crimeless or nearly crimeless society. Nevertheless, the Soviet crime rate is, more than six decades after the revolution, embarrassingly high—so much so that Soviet criminologists felt compelled to invent an auxiliary explanation: criminal behavior in the Soviet Union is an outcome of "survivals" of the bourgeois past in the Soviet minds.

However, even if removal of all these social ills were effective in preventing crime, we would be unable to remove the majority of them anyway and none of them easily and quickly. In particular, in view of the amount of crime in the United States, it is hardly possible to insulate everyone from associations with criminals and juvenile delinquents. It is equally impossible to "supply the missing 'parental affection' and restore to the child consistent discipline supported by a stable and loving family."[33] However much anomie, as claimed by Merton, may be responsible for a high proportion of criminal behavior, it would be difficult to "ask lower-class people to teach their children to strive for lower-class jobs only," to introduce a "caste system," or "to level all occupations."[34] If the Marxists had been correct—if a radical change of the socioeconomic system had been able to bring a crimeless society—it would be difficult to convince the American public that we can implement the ideal without destruction of free institutions. Thus, the attempt to solve the crime problem by removing broad "social causes" of criminal behavior is utopian. It was long ago ridiculed by Popper: "How far should we get if, instead of introducing laws and police force, we approached the problem of criminality 'scientifically', i.e., by trying to find out what precisely are the causes of crime. . . . It is as if one insisted that it is unscientific to wear an overcoat when it is cold; and that we should rather study the causes of cold weather, and remove them. Or, perhaps, that lubricating is unscientific, since we should rather find out the causes of friction and remove them.''[35]

There is only one method of efficient and prompt dealing with the crime problem, and this is proper administration of criminal justice. Somewhat paradoxically, this method eliminates the "causes" of crime as much as any one of the social reforms just mentioned. After all, the poverty of justice administration is an important "cause"—a factor contributing to many, if not all, kinds of criminal behavior. The factor operates mainly through the medium of the psychological process analyzed in the first part of this book: it destroys the educative power of criminal punishments. (It also operates, though much less forcefully, by destroying their deterrent power.) There is one critical difference, however, between this factor and the many others: it can be removed in a relatively easy way—it is much easier to improve the system of criminal punishments than to eliminate such assumed determinants of crime as lack of parental love, anomie, private property, social inequality, racial discrimination, unemployment, or density of population in urban areas. That is why the idea of eliminating all these determinants instead of improving criminal justice is not only fallacious but harmful; by influencing attitudes of judges, prosecutors, and others who carry out the criminal process, it undermines the educative force of criminal law and thus contributes to the great amount of crime. The implications of the fallacy go further than that, however. High crime rates are themselves a force hindering solution of many grave social problems. As I said earlier, they greatly increase the amount of suffering; are an important factor in the socioeconomic decline of the cities; make lives of the urban poor particularly deplorable (especially in the slum and the ghetto); and, by arousing widespread fear, bring setbacks in the process of racial integration. Thus, it is not only wrong to assume that solution of general social problems is the optimal implement for crime control. Rather the opposite is true. We can best control crime by improving criminal justice, and once we succeed in this,

73

the decrease of crime will itself become a major step toward an alleviation of the broader social ills.

Psychological Fallacy: Treatment

The belief that treatment and rehabilitation of criminals should replace punishment constitutes another component of the antipunitive philosophy. The belief comes from a variety of sources. First, it is an expression of a humanitarian and utilitarian stand against inflicting pain: criminal punishment, especially imprisonment, results in severe suffering. Moreover, the punishment is, to a large extent, applied as a retribution, and since the border between retribution and revenge is blurred, its opponents denounce the vindictiveness. Furthermore, they find strong support for their stand in the widespread assumption that attitudes of criminals (and of potential criminals, as if we were able to identify them in advance) can be changed by use of nonpunitive means at our disposal. Once we change the attitudes, the actual and potential criminals will refrain from wrongdoing, and thus the crime problem will be solved.

Psychiatrists, especially of the psychoanalytical brand, are most influential here. Many of them profess thorough psychic determinism: the criminal is driven toward crime by unconscious motivations that he is unable to control, and this makes punishing him not only inhuman but senseless. Criminal tendencies come, in particular, from the innate, destructive aggressiveness of the Id ("the human being enters the world as a criminal"[36]), if, due to a faulty Superego development, the aggressiveness is uninhibited. Among the more specific criminogenic forces there are infantile regression, uncontrollable sexual drives, inveterate guilt complexes producing an urge to commit crimes just to get punished and thus atone for the guilt, and the need to act out emotional conflicts—for example, masculinity-femininity conflict, Oedipal and Electra conflicts, conflicting desires for self-destruction and self-preservation.

74

All these psychological disorders, resulting mainly from early childhood experiences, are not, "according to the prevalent understanding of the words . . . a disease," but they could and *"should* be treated," as if they were.[37] The treatment should consist in "education, medication, counseling, training,"[38] most importantly in various kinds of psychotherapy: in putting, by free association, the criminogenic motivations out of unconsciousness, in group psychotherapy and in nondirective counseling—all this applied with love, which "is the touchstone," and with hope, which "is just as important as love in the therapeutic attitude."[39]

To support this antipunitive stand, its advocates use functioning of prisons as another important argument: prisons demoralize the inmates—they operate as if they were schools of crime. An adult, and even more so an adolescent, who enters the prison as an incidental offender has a high chance of becoming a hard-core criminal before release, and a habitual offender finds his habit reinforced.

There is a peculiar paradox in this. The very idea of treatment was introduced long ago into the heart of the American prison system, and many hopeful attempts have been made to change the prisons from punitive into rehabilitative institutions. They range from the early efforts of the Pennsylvania Quakers, who tried to reform wrongdoers by meditation in solitude, to the various programs of individual and group psychotherapy, often supplemented by educational and vocational training. The strong belief in the effectiveness of the programs became, as we saw, a rationale for indeterminate sentences and a partial rationale for the broad judicial sentencing discretion.[40]

The belief is unwarranted, however, and the programs are a failure; there is no evidence that they rehabilitate the convicts. This is particularly true of all kinds of psychotherapy—by far the most frequently used implement of treatment.[41] Some writers explain its ineffectiveness by its coercive application: the programs are most often compulsory, going through them is perceived by the inmates as a prerequisite for parole, and "psychotherapy, particu-

75

larly if it is of the psychoanalytical variety, must be voluntarily entered into . . . if it is to be effective."[42] However, it is rather the intrinsic deficiency of psychoanalysis and psychotherapy than their wrong use that explains the failure—an issue to which I shall return.

The prison not only fails to rehabilitate the convict, but it also, as its critics claim, corrupts him. Purely physical conditions of many antiquated prisons, overcrowding, idleness, abuse of power by prison guards, and abuse of many convicts by the most ruthless inmates—assault, extortion, and homosexual rape by fellow prisoners—contribute to the corruption. What contributes most, however, is the association with and influence by the criminals there. The convict becomes isolated from the outside world and spends his entire time in the company of lawbreakers. He adjusts to them and learns their criminal techniques and, most importantly, their criminal attitudes.[43] The younger he is, the more expedient is the learning; that is why juveniles, once convicted, get most easily demoralized by the company of their delinquent inmates. On top of that, the very stigma of being convicted begets, in society at large, reactions that, after release, additionally hamper adjustment to the noncriminal world.[44]

Thus, prisons "make their inhabitants worse, not better,"[45] and this provides another reason why, according to its advocates, treatment should replace punishment, especially incarceration. Some of them make qualified recommendations and suggest broad, but not complete, decriminalization: "the criminal justice system should be used only as a last resort in the control of undesirable conduct."[46] Many others sound stronger. "The American prison system makes no sense. Prisons have failed as . . . . rehabilitative institutions . . . and should be abolished."[47] "The principle of *no* punishment cannot allow of any exception; it must apply in every case."[48] What should be done is providing for "effective treatment for offenders" outside of any penal institutions.[49]

This mixture of ideas—the humanitarian and utilitarian stand, belief in feasibility of rehabilitation, and growing knowledge of criminogenic effects of imprisonment—has strongly contributed to the intermittence of criminal punishment. Under the impact of these ideas the courts are more inclined to let offenders go free, in particular by extensively granting probation with subsequent supervision, psychotherapy, community corrections, counseling, and other programs for the probationers. A particularly broad variety of nonpunitive programs, combined with probation or otherwise, has been devised for juvenile lawbreakers—community treatment, milieu therapy, skill development, and treatment in residential group centers, with Provo, Highfields, Silverlake, and California Community Treatment Program among those best known.

The frequent substitution of these adult and adolescent programs for imprisonment has recently come under growing criticism; the effectiveness of the programs has been challenged, and the failure to systematically convict wrongdoers has been widely denounced as returning the thugs to the streets and destroying whatever deterrent force the criminal sanctions have. The challenge to the effectiveness—the discovery that "almost none of the programs can be said to have succeeded"[50] and the general assertion of the "fallacy of the individual treatment model"[51]—is particularly strong. To be sure, the lawbreakers who go through any of the programs have a better chance of rehabilitation than those convicted—conviction demoralizes the most, and, when compared to imprisonment, the programs look as if they were a success.[52] However, none of the many experimental and quasi-experimental studies that have been conducted provides convincing evidence that the programs are more helpful in rehabilitating the lawbreaker than letting him go free and untreated,[53] and this implies that they do not work effectively.

And indeed, how could the programs work? Their effective implementation requires prior knowledge about how each program would operate, and the knowledge is not there; none of the programs is implemented as an application of a viable theory. The theories on which the programs are based are predominantly psychiatric and especially psychoanalytical. Unfortunately, much of psychiatry should be placed in "the category of pseudoscience,"[54] and this is particularly true of psychoanalysis. To be sure, many of Freud's insights and ideas hold a mark of true greatness, and it would be difficult to overestimate their intellectual impact on both his followers and adversaries. Still, his metapsychology is metaphysical: owing to its vagueness, it "can always be so manipulated that it escapes refutation no matter what the well established facts may be."[55] (This does not mean that it is valueless; if we accept falsifiability as the demarcation line of scientific knowledge, a large part of the most important human ideas fall into the category of metaphysics, and many of them—Freudian ideas included— may become scientific, once made precise enough to be tested.) Consequently, the theory, at least in its present shape, does not provide grounds for effective action. The conclusions drawn from it to explain various clinical cases are often instances of a revolutionary imagination. The conclusions are even more fanciful when the theory is being used to explain and remedy individual cases of criminal behavior. For instance:

A fifty-year old bachelor in Wisconsin murdered two middle-aged women, dissected and multilated their bodies, and then began desecrating graves of middle-aged women . . . . He was the son of a groceryman, and . . . as a child . . . used to watch . . . the bloody procedure [at the butchershop department]. He was very much attached to his mother and was never interested in any other women. Twelve years after his mother's death, he more or less accidentally shot and killed a middle-aged woman. He took her body home to his house and kept it, not quite certain how to dispose of it. After that he began to rob graves, always selecting female corpses and always taking them home to keep them with him in the house . . . . [S]ome of the deep unconscious meanings of this strange behavior [are clear]. His mother, whom he strove to "keep," was originally a very powerful, dominant woman . . . When she had a stroke and was partially paralyzed, this particular son took care of her personally and attended her until her death, which depressed him terribly. Afterward he kept thinking he heard her voice calling him. The mixture of his love of her and his need for her, and his buried hate and fear of her, was clearly shown in his fantastic, irrational reconstruction of the earlier home situation.[56]

And, in words of the same psychiatrist, one of his patients

was a great hunter, but only of one species of animal. . . . He often told me what great lust he had for killing swiftly and continually. "I have often wondered why I had it in for them so," he used to tell me, "but I just like to see them die and know that I caused it. In the course of his psychoanalytic reflections it suddenly occurred to him one day that his father's given name coincided—in another language—with the name of the animals that he so ruthlessly slaughtered. More than that, his father had once borne a nickname that referred to this same species, and confirming this he had a dream in which the target at which he was aiming with a deadly weapon turned into his father's face. He could no longer doubt whom he had been so eager to kill, over and over again, all his life.[57]

It is not surprising that treatment based on such notions is ineffective.[58] To be sure, not all the rehabilitative efforts are of the psychoanalytical variety; there are also other ideas, such as behavior modification, chemotherapy, or psychosurgery, but these are implements of very narrow application, novelties of uncertain effectiveness, or morally and constitutionally dubious schemes. For instance, advocates of behavior modification claim some success in conditioning drug addicts, alcoholics, or homosexuals (all of whom, as I have already indicated, should be out of concern of criminal justice anyway);[59] but how to persuade bank robbers, burglars, kidnappers, or terrorists to change their ways by application of unpleasant noise, nauseating tablets, or mild electric shocks? Psychosurgery, particularly destruction of some brain cells (as well as chemotherapy, if used to permanently change some components of the lawbreaker's nervous system) have old predecessors. Many societies have practiced removal of the physical prerequisites of crime—by cutting off the thief's hand or the slanderer's tongue or by castrating those guilty of illicit intercourse. Psychosurgery and chemotherapy, however less cruel, still evoke, because of their Orwellian flavor and risks of injury and personal-

79

ity change, strong ethical and aesthetic apprehensions.[60] It would be imprudent to preclude entirely their eventual broader use.[61] However, the widespread use is infeasible today or in the predictable future. It presupposes great progress in science, especially in biochemistry and neurophysiology, and a favorable outcome of difficult constitutional battles.

What then, if anything, could be done to treat criminals effectively? "Does nothing work?" asks one of the most penetrating analysts.[62] The answer, at least in the present state of scientific knowledge, is disappointing: we do not know how to rehabilitate large numbers of wrongdoers. True, we can succeed in individual cases. For instance, psychotherapy may sometimes be effective, not thanks to the validity of psychoanalytical theory, but rather as a persuasion facilitated by clarification of options and by a rewarding feeling of being consoled or being able to unburden oneself. Moreover, we can succeed in placing a very limited number of individual lawbreakers in exemplary primary groups and exposing them for long periods to the familiar process of persuasive communications and persuasive punishments and reinforcements, which operate within the group. For instance, a single delinquent juvenile, if admitted for years to an isolated boarding school filled with nondelinquent students and superior staff, would have a good chance of getting rehabilitated. For obvious reasons, however, only few can be treated this way; an attempt to treat many would, in this instance, bring a delinquent subculture to the school, reinforcing criminal attitudes of its members and endangering the morale of others. The method may therefore have considerable potential only in societies with very low crime rates. In the United States, however, or in any crime-ridden society, it is infeasible, just like all other methods already discussed. Thus the conclusion is clear: we are unable to treat criminals on a large scale. Consequently, it would be an error to make of their treatment the main goal and of themselves the main addressees of crime control policy.

The main goal and addressees and implements of the viable

policy have been identified in the first part of this book. The policy should be addressed to the society at large and aimed at its moral education. It should use justly and systematically enforced criminal sanctions as the implement. From this standpoint, the ideology of treatment, however well intended, is not only fallacious but harmful. By contributing to reluctant enforcement of punishments, it undermines the educative power of criminal justice and thus, instead of helping, hinders efforts at preventing crime.

Constitutional Constraints

Constitutional constraints on obtaining evidence are—besides leniency—the other major factor contributing to the uncertainty of criminal law enforcement. To make systematic enforcement possible, acquisition of evidence must be reasonably easy—only then will the truth be provable in an overwhelming majority of criminal prosecutions. This is not, however, the case in this country; restrictive norms, introduced in particular to protect constitutional rights, make the acquisition difficult. The norms prohibit use of various means of obtaining evidence, and the prohibitions are sanctioned primarily by exclusionary rule. Evidence gathered in violation of them may not be used in court, even if it clearly proves the incriminating truth.

The number of prohibitions sanctioned by exclusionary rule is considerable; they match a substantial part of the Bill of Rights guarantees. The majority of them are directed to police. They include, in particular, the bans on illegal arrest, on illegal search and seizure, and on infringements of the privilege against self-incrimination and of the right to counsel. The scope of each of these prohibitions has been persistently broadened, especially under the Warren Court's constitutional construction. Whenever any of the prohibitions gets broken, the exclusionary rule cuts deep; it brings suppression not only of the proof directly acquired in an illegal way but also of the derivative evidence. The suppression had long been considered by the Court as a "deterrent safe-guard"[63] against the encroachments and, moreover, as an "imperative of judicial integrity."[64]

The prohibitions and exclusions bring about important benefits. They enhance not only the constitutional rights of suspects but also the liberty of all of us; in particular, they prevent placing "the liberty of every man in the hands of every petty officer."[65] Some of them help protect the innocent from conviction and thus avert the gravest injustice. All of them provide for greater fairness of the criminal process and consequently enhance the prestige of administration of justice. In Earl Warren's words, "[n]o general respect for . . . the law . . . can well be expected without judicial recognition of the paramount need for . . . eminently fair . . . criminal procedures."[66]

Whatever their value, the prohibitions, and in particular the exclusionary rule with its broad coverage of derivative evidence, impede certainty of punishment. It is no wonder that the rule has often been criticized, though rather for its negative impact on individual and general deterrence than for the reasons endorsed in this book. Chief Justice Burger's complaint is characteristic: "For more than 55 years this Court has enforced a rule under which evidence of undoubted reliability and probative value has been suppressed and excluded from criminal cases. . . . This . . . rule is unique to American jurisprudence."[67] Its binding force means that "[t]he criminal is to go free because the constable has blundered."[68]

Unfortunately, as long as police cannot be trusted, the exclusionary rule will probably have to stay with us. True, the rule is either unknown or has very limited application under the laws of other open societies, in particular of Canada, Britain, and various Western European countries. In many of them, however, the police are better supervised, more professional, and in some of them, especially in Britain, traditionally honest. In spite of much progress, this is not necessarily the case in this country, and such means of controlling police as criminal prosecutions, tort actions, or injunctions have been clearly insufficient.[69] That is why, according to the prevailing opinion, and in particular in view of the Court, "only . . . exclusionary rule . . . can be an effective sanction to assure that law enforcement authorities will respect the accused's constitutional right[s]."[70]

The legitimacy of the rule does not mean, however, that all the prohibitions sanctioned by it are reasonable. Their scope, as I mentioned, has been greatly increased by the Court, and there is one area of critical importance where the increase went clearly too far. The area consists in police interrogations and confessions, and I shall focus on them.

My basic premise here is that early interrogation of suspects constitutes a particularly valuable implement for acquisition of evidence. When apprehended, a guilty suspect is usually unaware how much the police know of his behavior. This is one reason why elicitation of a confession may be possible only at this stage of the procedure. The elicitation provides a simple means for obtaining derivative evidence to eventually prove the suspect's guilt. It is often the only means: "Despite modern advances in the technology of crime detection, offenses frequently occur about which things cannot be made to speak," claimed Justice Frankfurter in *Culombe v. Connecticut,*[71] where police were confronted with two corpses and an infant as their only informants.

And where there cannot be found innocent human witnesses to such offenses, nothing remains—if police investigation is not to be balked before it has fairly begun—but to seek out possibly guilty witnesses and ask them questions. . . . The questions which these suspected witnesses are asked may serve to clear them. They may serve . . . to lead the police to other suspects. . . . Or they may become the means by which the persons questioned are themselves made to furnish proofs which will eventually send them to prison or death. In any event, whatever its outcome, such questioning is often indispensable to crime detection."[72]

How to elicit confession from a criminal who—as is most often the case—does not want to confess spontaneously when interrogated? The crucial step is to persuade him to start talking.

83

CRIMINAL PUNISHMENT

This does not imply that a legal obligation to answer questions should be imposed on him. To be sure, the idea of that duty is not unthinkable: "Justice . . . would not perish if the accused were subject to a duty to respond to orderly inquiry."[73] Acceptance of a duty to speak could, however, easily bring us too far. It might be followed by belief that the suspect, if obliged to speak, is also duty bound to tell the truth, even the incriminating truth, and that the duty is subject to sanctions. This would bring us dangerously close to inquisitorial practices.

To persuade the suspect to speak, much less than that is needed. There seem to be three minimal prerequisites for this. First, the police must be allowed to pursue an energetic interrogation. Second, the suspect must not be supported by anyone who would advise him to be silent; this implies, in particular, no counsel's assistance at interrogation: "any lawyer worth his salt—in Justice Jackson's words—will tell the suspect . . . to make no statement to police under any circumstances."[74] Third, if the suspect refuses to speak, the prosecution must be free to comment at trial on his refusal, and, most importantly, the police must be free to tell him, during the interrogation, that the comment might be made. As I said, all this does not imply a duty to speak or to tell the truth; the suspect would be legally free to keep silent or speak and, when speaking, to tell the truth or to lie. Once, however, he opts for lying, there almost always is, under a skillful interrogation, a good chance for him to be confronted with the lies and eventually to confess.

The just listed prerequisites had been present in criminal procedure until the mid-1960s. In particular, constitutional constraints on energetic police interrogation were limited to the general demand that confessions be, under totality of circumstances, voluntary. The demand (misleading, because of its psychological wording) meant a due process requirement of fairness in taking confessions and was aimed at two partially converging goals—that evidence by trustworthy and that even the guilty would not be incriminated by indecent means.[75] Clearly, this requirement did not prohibit the police from warning the suspect that his silence might be commented upon at trial (unless, owing to specific circumstances of a case, the warning ran against ''voluntariness''). Furthermore, neither this requirement—nor the sixth amendment as traditionally construed—provided for the counsel's necessary assistance at the interrogation.[76]

However, the ''voluntariness-totality of circumstances'' test fell, in the 1960s, under sharp criticism. It apparently provided an elusive standard;[77] the case-by-case process of its sharpening never furnished a clear guide, and this lack of clarity brought about frequent challenges of state court decisions that resulted in an overburdening of the federal judiciary. More importantly, the test was inadequate because the courts were unable to ascertain what occurred behind the closed door of the interrogation room. Police often resorted to various dubious means, including deception and even physical force to obtain confessions.[78] A suspect's plea of coercion was, however, rarely successful because the police interrogations were usually unsupervised.

The police practices were considered as abusive, as an infringement of the suspect's dignity, and as a debasement of the administration of criminal justice. In addition, they entailed a risk of unfounded conviction, especially of the poor and the inexperienced.[79] Moreover, the Supreme Court, because of its workload, was able to review but a minute portion of the procedural shortcomings.[80]

For these reasons the Court provided some general remedies in a series of decisions. First, having abandoned the ''voluntariness-totality of circumstances'' criterion in *Malloy v. Hogan*,[81] it applied the self-incrimination clause of the fifth amendment to the states and opened the way for applying the clause to state-run custodial interrogation.[82] Furthermore, building on a series of prior cases,[83] it applied the counsel guarantee of the sixth amendment to the interrogation in *Escobedo v. Illinois*. Finally, it laid down a whole set of remedial provisions in *Miranda v. Arizona*.[84] First, it explicitly extended the fifth amendment privilege to the interrogation and thus clarified the suspect's right to remain silent. Second, it reiterated the *Escobedo* holding that the suspect has a right to consult with his lawyer prior to questioning. The *Miranda* holding, however, was based on the self-incrimination clause of the fifth amendment rather than on the sixth amendment right to counsel. Third, it established the suspect's right to have counsel present during the entire interrogation. Fourth, it gave indigent suspects the right to a lawyer without charge. Moreover, it maintained that the prosecution may not comment at trial on the suspect's silence,[85] and the view has been upheld in later decisions.[86]

The *Miranda* Court anticipated that the majority of suspects would be unaware of their rights and that the police could easily exploit this ignorance. Thus, for these rights to be implemented, suspects had to know about them. The Court held, therefore, that the police have a duty to warn the suspect of all four rights prior to any questioning. In the absence of the warnings and an express waiver with full understanding, a suspect's confession or any other statement is to be excluded from the evidence at trial.

If faithfully implemented, the dictates of *Miranda* can only result in the virtual disappearance of confessions. Although a suspect may confess when confronted by the police with conclusive evidence gathered beforehand, the confession would be useless. A confession has value only if its absence makes collecting other incriminating evidence difficult or impossible. *Miranda,* if fully implemented, will enable the suspect to understand this situation. Thus, whenever a confession is of value, he will not confess, unless he wants to do so irrespective of the consequences.[87]

The disappearance of confessions would seriously impair the investigation of crimes in which little independent evidence could be found. The potential impairment has spawned an immediate widespread criticism of the decision. The dissenting justices in *Miranda* felt that the decision would "return a killer, a rapist or other criminal to the streets," weaken the deterrent force of sanctions, and thus "have a corrosive effect on the criminal law as an effective device to prevent crime."[88] This view has been supported by both lawyers and laymen. Furthermore, polling on a related issue suggests that a large majority of Americans sympathize with the view of the dissenting justices.[89] Most importantly, this view has been widely adopted by police and is reflected in their behavior.

Several empirical studies have assessed the impact of *Miranda* on the police. Studies conducted in New Haven,[90] Washington, D.C.,[91] and Denver[92] are the most reliable.[93] These studies reveal that the police evaded *Miranda* warnings in a majority of the interrogations under scrutiny. Moreover, the warnings given indicate a grudging adherence to the letter of *Miranda* rather than genuine compliance with its requirements. To avoid the sanction of the exclusionary rule, the warnings are voiced in such a way that the suspect is unable to understand their meaning. Furthermore, if a suspect grasps some of his rights, and if his exercise of them may cripple interrogation in a serious case, the police are inclined to question him persistently against his expressed will[94] and to divert his attention if he shows an interest in finding a lawyer.[95]

This behavior of interrogators has sometimes been explained by the conflict of roles imposed on them by the Supreme Court. *Miranda* requires a detective to perform the impossible by acting both as interrogator and counsel for the defense.[96] This explanation, however, is incomplete. The police feel that strict adherence to the *Miranda* rulings would cripple systematic law enforcement, and they rightly consider the systematic enforcement an important social need. Thus, they evade the rulings to meet the need.[97] Moreover, police also feel that the rulings run "counter to our ordinary standards of morality."[98] The belief that the suspect ought to give true answers to an orderly police interrogation is widespread,[99] and attitudes of police officers are, like anyone else's, influenced by widespread moral sentiment.

Thus compromised by police, the *Miranda* warnings work badly. Because of their frequent evasion, the warnings do not provide sufficient constraint against police abuse. Consequently, the values underlying their pronouncement remain unprotected. This result was anticipated by Justice Harlan in his dissent from *Miranda*. He argued that interrogators inclined to use third-degree tactics could easily give unclear warnings or coerce waivers and thereby protect their tactics.[100] Indeed, post-*Miranda* empirical data reveal that police abuse happens at interrogation. Its exact scope cannot be easily assessed, but it is not exceptional. Empirical studies report that the police use a variety of threats to compel confessions. The threat used most often is that of combining several charges or of charging the suspect with past crimes.[101] The police also threaten some suspects with a heavier charge, a heavier penalty, or excessive bond.[102] Another tactic is to tell the suspect that his family or friends will be in trouble if he does not talk.[103] Finally, to coerce a confession, some police apparently resort to physical force.[104]

Thus the evasion of the *Miranda* requirements is widespread. Nevertheless, and most importantly for these considerations, it is far from total. This fact is apparently ignored by commentators who assert that the impact of *Miranda* on law enforcement is negligible.[105] Quite to the contrary, these commentators' own discoveries reveal that the *Miranda* requirements impair systematic application of punishment. One study, for example, discovered that the *Miranda* warnings resulted in a 10 percent decrease in the willingness of suspects to talk.[106] The same study revealed that in 7 percent of the cases the warnings impeded solution of the crime,[107] and in 11 percent of the cases with accomplices, the warnings hindered the identification or implication of accomplices.[108] In addition, the warnings produced a 10 percent decrease in the clearance of crimes other than the crime under investigation.[109] Finally, the study showed that the suspects' silence enhanced their position in future plea bargaining. Whenever the absence of a confession makes the prosecutor's case weaker, he is anxious to avoid trial. Thus plea bargaining resulted in a reduced charge in 31 percent of the cases in which the defendant confessed but in 62 percent of those in which he was silent.[110] This fact suggests that the warnings make an indirect contribution to the uncertainty and inconsistency of punishment by giving suspects more to bargain with.

These statistics are quite impressive. Moreover, their significance should be appraised historically. In the present state of the administration of criminal justice in the United States, they suggest the acceleration of a harmful trend. New Haven investigators said in 1966 that most suspects were unable to grasp the meaning of *Miranda* warnings.[111] Only a minority of suspects knew their rights when arrested and immediately refused to talk or asked for a lawyer.[112] Knowledge of the *Miranda* requirements is, however, spreading rapidly, especially among potential law breakers.[113] This trend can only result in an ever-increasing impairment of systematic law enforcement.

In summary, the *Miranda* requirements have resulted in a compromise practice that is detrimental to both the suspect and society. On the one hand, they do not effectively protect the values that they are supposed to protect. On the other hand, by letting criminals go free, they further weaken punitive certainty and thus undermine the educative power of criminal justice. Indeed, however well intended by the libertarians who devised them, they make very bad law from either perspective.

Part Three

THE IMPLICATIONS

INTRODUCTORY REMARKS

THE IMPLICATIONS OF the preceding analysis are clear: a number of changes should be introduced into the legal system to provide for justice (especially for consistency) and for certainty of punishment. The claim of just and certain punishments is not new, of course. What is new is the emphasis on its specific reason—the educative effects of its implementation rather than the often stressed ultimate value of justice or teleology of general and individual deterrence. The educative effect will—and this is the basic inference from the first part of this book—bring about a far-reaching decline of criminal behavior.

This inference does not constitute an overestimation of the role of law and legal sanctions. In particular, the inference does not mean that we can, simply by use of criminal law, extensively shape the morality of society; criminal law can be only one of the many forces that influence moral judgments.[1] If properly applied, however, criminal law is a powerful force, and it may be used for crime control in a relatively easy manner—much easier than the

93

IMPLICATIONS

sweeping reforms of various social institutions implied by many crime-causation theorists.

The changes that must be introduced into the legal system should be limited to the necessary minimum: any major legal modification, in particular in criminal law and procedure, entails a risk of unexpected side-effects. It is largely due to this risk that piecemeal, empirical reforms have always been characteristic of the development of American law. Quite obviously, however, some of the needed changes must run deep. Furthermore, the administration of criminal justice constitutes a complex system of interdependent behavior. Consequently, changing some of its components may imperil the operation of the others and thus make adaptive changes in the others necessary. All this implies an overhaul of considerable proportions. The basics of the overhaul will be derived from the preceding chapters and outlined in the chapters to follow.

Chapter Four

THE CRIMES

CRIMES THE PUNISHMENT for which runs against the actual or clearly emerging moral sentiment of the society should be removed from criminal codes. Two instances of such crimes—homosexual behavior and drug abuse—were analyzed earlier. How can the removal be implemented? This depends on its sociolegal implications, and the implications differ from one crime to another. Sometimes the removal brings only an eradication of injustice and no other consequences, especially no harmful effects. Then the process of decriminalization is simple: it may consist in a flat abolishment of the penalty, legislative or even court made, without any further changes in other elements of the legal system. This is how the problem of homosexual acts between consenting adults in private could be solved. There are crimes, however, for which, owing to the complexity of the social issues involved and the interdependence of various parts of the law, the penalty may be abolished only by comprehensive legislation; otherwise, disruptions in various components of the legal system and of the broader social system would occur. This is exactly the case with the second of the cited instances—abolishment of penalties for possession and use of narcotics by the addict; to show how difficult the decriminalizing process may be, I shall comment on this now in some detail.

A flat ban on the penalties would result in harmful consequences, all of them clear in the light of the preceding analysis of drug abuse. First, it would legalize use of narcotics without providing for any supervision of their use. Second, it would leave the crucial problem of drug supplies unresolved. Third, its logic would carry over to various kinds of acquisitive behavior. Those who are powerless to avoid using a drug may be equally powerless to avoid doing whatever is necessary to acquire it. Thus, the ban on penalties could easily become extended to "all other crimes—bank robberies, street muggings, burglaries—which can be shown to be the product of the same drug-craving compulsion." [2] Indeed, the claim of this extension has been made by Judge Bazelon, a staunch supporter of the ban. [3] These are some of the reasons why the courts, however hesitatingly, did not simply abolish the penalties. Instead, they recommended that all the pertinent "ultimate problems of law and policy should be addressed by the Congress" [4] and by legislatures of the states.

How should the lawmakers address the issue? In the light of the preceding comments at least one essential component of the necessary change seems to be obvious: the use of narcotics by the addicts should be permitted with a lawful supply, at low cost or, if necessary, free. This does not mean making acquisition of heroin legal for all who wish it; but it means strictly supervising its administration in well-checked clinics (or by licensed doctors). It would require prior examination of each prospective recipient and, once his dependence has been established, maintaining him with an amount of the drug sufficient to keep him free of withdrawal symptoms. Heroin maintenance could be replaced by other, more appropriate drugs only for those who might be persuaded to accept a substitute voluntarily. The most significant substitute currently available is methadone. It is in several respects superior to heroin. It can be taken orally and less frequently than heroin; thus, its administration is easier and cheaper. Since no tolerance develops to its effects, its dosage can be maintained indefinitely on the same level. Its small dosages remove heroin withdrawal symptoms, whereas its high dosages establish a cross-tolerance to all opiates and thus prevent emergence of the heroin-produced euphoria.[5] However, only a fraction of the addicts will voluntarily accept methadone maintenance. It is attractive predominantly to those older users who, being tired of the heroin cycle, are inclined to accept a noneuphoric substitute.

Neither heroin nor methadone maintenance can cure the dependent user—the latter "merely transfers his . . . dependence from one drug to another."[6] However, effective treatment of a large proportion of the addicts is, in the current state of knowledge, an impossible objective. The effectiveness of voluntary programs—like various kinds of therapy or detoxification—seems to be negligible[7]; it is even smaller if compulsion is being applied.[8] Future discoveries, pharmacological, psychological or some other, may change this. For instance, discovery of new "antagonist drugs"[9] or other techniques of aversive conditioning may make a universally working inhibition feasible. Until this happens, curing the addict cannot be considered as the main objective of a reasonable legal policy, and it is not so considered by the narcotic maintenance program advocated here. (However, the program may and should be supplemented by persuasion to undergo treatment whenever there may be any chance of success.) Thus, it is a program of resignation: it considers the majority of opiate addiction cases as hopeless. Nevertheless, once introduced, the program will be instrumental in achieving two realistic objectives: it will remove injustice in dealing with addicts and help eliminate acquisitive crime.

There is also a third objective, because of the harms engendered by addiction: to prevent recruitment of new addicts. Its achievement presumes an effective attack on the heroin black mar-

IMPLICATIONS

ket. The attack may concentrate on one or more of the three targets, each of them essential for the market's operation: the original foreign production, the subsequent supply by the dealers, and the acquisition by users. Concentrating on the first is tempting. An effective deal with foreign governments eliminating poppy fields or heroin laboratories would be the simplest way out. It requires, however, an amount of power that may not be there. China was trying to use a similar method and lost to Britain in the Opium Wars. Its use is also difficult for the United States; there are a number of opium-growing countries, and an eventual success in dealing with one of them does not preclude production's shifting to the others. Efforts should rather focus on establishment of a working international system of control, but this may be hopeless in today's international order.

The activity of dealers—importers, wholesalers, small traffickers, doctors who abuse the trust—should become the main target. The eradication of the activity will be made easier by the establishment of the narcotic maintenance program. The users who want the drug most will get it from legitimate sources. However, there will still be demand for black market supplies on the part of novice users and, unless the maintenance program is arranged efficiently, on the part of the addicts who either want to supplement their maintenance doses or did not register for the program. That is why criminal sanctions are needed. They should be applied to the dealers in a just and systematic way. The requirement of justice means here, in particular, that the law would grade the sanctions according to the harmfulness of the offense, with the highest penalties aimed at large-scale heroin dealers. The claim of systematic enforcement indicates the abandonment of the present system, which apprehends a small fraction of the sellers and returns many of those apprehended to the streets. A vigorous pursuit of the policy of arrests and incarceration is needed. (This policy would coincide with the more general idea of punitive certainty.)

How should we deal with the third component of the black market—buyers of heroin for their own use? Some writers believe that the users are "the key element in the heroin market" and recommend directing "law enforcement . . . at the user rather than the dealer."[10] If this implies harsher penalties for users than for dealers, the recommendation is wrong; there is much more turpitude in the activity of the sellers (who harm others) than of the users (who harm themselves). This is the main reason why sellers rather than users should be made the principal target. On the other hand, milder penalties for users, however less important, are not unwarranted. They may be justified by legal paternalism,[11] and they may indirectly help in combating dealers. They would have to be enforced mainly under the guise of penalties for possession, and a possession offense is expedient in prosecuting the seller. Most importantly, under the scheme proposed here, punishment would be inflicted on the not-yet-addicted novice users and on addicts who resort to illegal acquisition even though they have a legal alternative—that is, on those who do not act under irresistible drive and thus can be blamed for what they are doing.

The decriminalization proposal outlined here may bring doubts. It is in one important respect similar to the British system: it supports narcotic maintenance of dependent users. The maintenance, approved under the Rolleston Committee recommendations of 1926, has been considered a success, despite the increase of drug use in Britain in the 1960s. It has been also advocated in this country. However, its many opponents claim that its relative success in England does not assure it will work in America.

They point, first, to the difference in numbers: the narcotics-dependent population in Britain has never exceeded 3000, whereas estimates in the United States range from 150,000 to 375,000.[12] This makes handling a maintenance program more difficult here. In particular, leakages of heroin and methadone, which have also troubled the British, would present a much greater danger in America. Moreover, the opponents stress most emphatically the broader sociocultural differences that may render the British experience irrelevant. The addicts in England today "are not as a rule from disadvantaged families [and] . . . minority

99

groups, and do not 'turn on' to blot out the economic despair of the ghetto.'' They are rather '' 'middle class dropouts' whose addiction . . . appears to have been motivated by the deliberate rejection of middle-class norms.''[13] This means that the British get addicted because of anxieties very different from those that push a young, lower class American to the use of heroin.[14] The difference is compounded by other cultural factors, like the law-abiding nature of an average Englishman. Thus, opponents of the maintenance program find reasons ''to believe that British and American addicts are sufficiently different so that an American clinic system would not attract as large a proportion of the total addict population as have the British clinics.''[15] Worse than that, they claim the program may be counterproductive: ''it is . . . hard to understand [why] the number of addicts . . . would be stabilized or reduced if heroin were made easier to get.''[16] Moreover, introduction of the program ''would remove some of the major hazards of becoming addicted and thus might increase the overall addict population.''[17] There is also a touch of sheer conservatism in this opposition: fear of unknown risks involved in any major policy change.

The fear is reasonable, and so are some of the more specific arguments. In particular, it is true that the large number of addicts makes administration of the maintenance program harder, and, to prevent leakages, stress may have to be put on administration of narcotics at the clinic rather than on prescriptions. However, the main argument of the opponents—the differential impact of the sociocultural differences—is a non sequitur. The differences mean only that social factors leading to addiction differ from England to America. Once addicted, however, every heroin user goes through a similar psycho-physiological driving experience, irrespective of the society he lives in. That is why there are major differences in motivation (and behavior) of experimenters and novice users from culture to culture, but not in the motivation of those already dependent. Consequently, a well-organized and easily accessible narcotic maintenance program, when offered in lieu of a hard acquisitive struggle, should equally attract the American, British, or any other addicts. This has been corroborated by a study of behavior, in Canada and in England, of a group of Canadian heroin users who moved to England in the 1960s.[18] Thus, the estimate that "heroin maintenance would presumably attract virtually all . . . the street addict population" in the United States[19] seems not to sound overoptimistic.

True, the maintenance would not solve the problem of beginners, and the American beginners may be more difficult to handle than many others. That is why the vigorous attack against the black market outlined here is necessary. Only the demanding combination of both narcotic maintenance (in lieu of blind narcotic prohibition) and energetic law enforcement would solve all the difficult issues involved—eliminate the injustice of the present system, eradicate acquisitive crime, and help prevent recruitment of users.

Drug abuse is only an instance. There are more crimes on the codes whose punishment may, owing to future changes in the moral climate, become unjust; some of them (for instance, prostitution)[20] will probably become unjust soon. The complexity of decriminalizing drug abuse by addicts should convey the gist of potential difficulties that, consequently, may await the legal draftsmen.

spect to every criminal offense they learn of, provided, of course, that the perpetrator can be located and that the offense seems provable. This does not imply a complete loss of decision-making power; the officers would still often have to interpret both the law and the encountered behavior to determine whether the behavior is criminal, and, if it is, they would have to estimate whether it can feasibly by proved. Furthermore, limiting police discretion does not necessarily imply that every perpetrator would have to be arrested. As will be stressed later, a broad use of fines should replace incarceration for minor offenses. With respect to serious crimes, interrogation or summons rather than arrest is the proper way of handling suspects, unless there is a probability of a suspect's fleeing, tampering with evidence, or continuing criminal behavior. Thus, limiting discretion means here only that no provable crime committed by someone who can be detected may simply be disregarded and its investigation set aside.

This change must be accompanied by limiting prosecutorial discretion. If the suspect's guilt may be expected to be proved in court, the prosecutor should be duty bound to charge him with the crime committed—at least when the crime is serious.[1] This duty would run clearly against the long and well-embedded tradition of powerful prosecutors whose right to decide whether to prosecute or not has been almost unrestricted and free from review. Some comparative lawyers claim that the enforcement of this duty would require a reshaping of the prosecutorial system along the European lines, making of it an agency of appointed career civil servants, each of them responsible hierarchically for their decisions.[2] This may be the optimal arrangement, but it is not the only arrangement feasible. To be sure, decisions of the prosecutors would have to be checked, but the checking can be done without establishing a rigidly structured bureaucracy. Their duty to prosecute systematically, as well as sanctions for breaking the duty, can be explicitly written into the law. The sanctions, including suspension from and forfeiture of the office and, conceivably, other penalties, could be imposed by courts, and the charges could be pressed by state attorneys general and, within the federal system, by the Attorney General of the United States.

The sweeping judicial discretion (or discretion of juries in those few states where they are given general sentencing powers) is, as the earlier comments should have made clear, particularly harmful, and so is the discretion of the administrative sentence-fixing bodies. The judicial discretion should be drastically limited and the administrative discretion eliminated. The elimination of the latter means an abolition of indeterminate sentences—a direction in which the law is already headed. The limitation of the former cannot but start with the introduction of one basic principle: an obligation of the judges to impose the prescribed punishment for every crime proved to have been committed. This would entail two major changes. First, it would remove judicial discretion about whether to punish criminals, including the removal of suspended sentences and probation. Secondly, the acceptance of the principle would make judges unable to arbitrarily select crimes for which they convict defendants; each defendant would have to be punished for the crime proved to have been committed. Thus, if the crime is unquestionably murder, the judge would break the law when imposing punishment prescribed for manslaughter—a requirement that is a commonplace under any legal system except ours.

All this implies limiting judicial discretion, not its disappearance. To be just, punishment must fit the amount of guilt, and since for any kind of crime the amount varies from case to case, there must be reasonable room left for discretionary gradation of punitive measures. The room can be provided only by sentencing alternatives and, in particular, sentencing ranges. They must not be excessively broad, however (for instance, punishment for a crime ranging from 1 year to life or to the death penalty[3]); the judge should fix penalties within the statutory boundaries of reasonable width.

The judicial fixing power does not imply arbitrariness; as I said, the judge should, within the statutory boundaries, select the

105

kind and measure of punishment that match the degree of the defendant's guilt. Thus, determining the degree becomes an important responsibility.

In the most general meaning the term *guilt* denotes our feeling of blameworthiness of past behavior. Thus, the degree of a defendant's guilt would be determined by our feeling of blameworthiness of his criminal act. By "our feeling" I understand here the feeling dominant in the society. This understanding does not assume (as I mentioned in a different context earlier)[4] a full uniformity of evaluations; the assumption, unwarranted in any large social group, would be evidently false in an open and pluralistic society of today. It assumes, however, a degree of consensus—a basic consensus not only about which acts deserve punishment[5] but also about the relative blameworthiness of those that do. In particular, there seems to be little doubt in America that, all other factors being equal, the more harmful a criminal act for others, the more blameworthy it is;[6] therefore, an aggravated battery that results in a permanent paralysis or blindness of the victim deserves more blame than an offense of the same kind where a finger was lost. There is also little doubt that the intensity of criminal intent or negligence, ranging from heinous willfulness in producing the criminal result to *dolus eventualis* to recklessness to carelessness, does influence the degree of blame deserved. Moreover, a large number of personal, social, and situational circumstances that may influence the degree can be added to a commonly acceptable list, such as the motives of the defendant, his behavior during the criminal act, his past (especially his past wrongdoing), the level of his mental development and emotional stability, his relationship with the victim, and the victim's behavior preceding the crime. This incomplete catalog implies how difficult the measurement of guilt may be—various judges, when dealing with a like case, can estimate differently the degree of blame that the society would have experienced if it had learned about the offense. That is why the judicial estimates must be made uniform, checked, and rectified when necessary. This can be best accomplished by the appellate review of sentences.

DISCRETION AND BARGAINING

The review, having been adopted by all other Western societies, is absent from the majority of American jurisdictions.[7] To be sure, it is always available if a sentence exceeds the statutory boundaries. If it does not, however, the majority of the state laws and the federal law do not provide for review on the exclusive ground of excessiveness of sentence. A few decisions to the contrary, where courts held excessive but legal penalties as violations of the eighth amendment,[8] refer to exceptional extremes and have not been universally accepted.[9]

The routine review of excessive sentences has been widely recommended in recent years. Its proponents consider it as "one step toward the rule of law in a quarter where lawless and unchecked power has reigned for too long,"[10] and demand that the review "should be available for all sentences imposed in cases where provision is made for review of the conviction."[11] These demands are limited, however; most often they refer only to excessively severe sentences, and not to those that are too lenient. With this limitation in mind, advocates of the review recommend that "[n]o reviewing court should be empowered to impose, or direct the imposition of, a sentence which results in an increase over the sentence imposed at the trial level."[12]

The limitation seems to be ill advised; the psychological considerations described earlier make it clear that both excessively severe and excessively lenient punishments are inconsistent, that is, unjust, and thus undermine the educative force of criminal law. That is why both should be reversible on appeal. This does not imply that *reformatio in peius* should be accepted—a possibility of aggravation of punishment following appeal by the defendant; the possibility might go too far in discouraging appeal by convicts.[13] What is being suggested here means only that both defense and prosecution should be allowed to appeal sentences—a solution adopted by most European states, and from time to time recommended also in this country, though for reasons different from mine.[14]

There are dangers in accepting this recommendation, most importantly a danger of courts' being flooded by frivolous appeals,

107

which would cause major additional costs and delays. The somewhat vague character of the issue involved provides ground for the danger; the amount of guilt is often unclear, and, consequently, there is no precise measure determining exactly how severe a penalty should be; only from some point on the punishment becomes intolerably severe or intolerably lenient.[15] Thus, the "abuse" of the right to appeal may be tempting, especially for defendants.

There is a way to avoid the danger. It consists, first, in limiting the effectiveness of the review to violations of justice that are gross enough to be obvious[16]—the limitation would make capricious appeals unpromising. Moreover, the appellate court should be duty bound, whenever possible, to affirm or modify the sentence on the record; only if necessary might a case be remanded for further proceeding and resentencing to the court *a quo*. Of course, the necessity of remanding would be rare under a system where only an obviously arbitrary sentence might be modified —the record from the court *a quo* and the stated reasons for its sentence would almost always make it clear whether an obvious arbitrariness occurred. Consequently, the review procedure would be brief and simple, and the danger of major additional costs and delays would be avoided.

I have mentioned stating the reasons for the sentence as an element of the suggested procedure. Without precise specification of the reasons, the decision whether to make an appeal would be difficult, as would be the review of the sentence by the appellate court. There are also other considerations that make an explanation of the sentence necessary. Being obliged to specify reasons, the sentencing judge becomes additionally motivated to make his thinking on the sentence precise and responsible. Moreover, and most importantly, pronouncement of reasons for the sentence enhances the persuasiveness of the court's communication. If the reasons are clearly and convincingly stated, the defendant and the observers will be much better impressed that he is being punished because his behavior was intrinsically wrong. The educative impact of this impression should be clear in the light of earlier considerations.

Removing Negotiated Pleas

The theoretical perspective accepted in this book, and the earlier description of plea negotiations, imply a brief and simple recommendation: plea bargaining should be prohibited. Its abolition has been implicitly proposed in preceding paragraphs: plea bargaining will automatically disappear once prosecutors and judges lose, respectively, discretion about whether to charge and convict, discretion about what to charge with and convict for, and discretion to recommend and grant leniency except for a low degree of guilt. Since plea bargaining undermines general deterrence and returns wrongdoers to the streets, its abolition had been recommended before, most forcefully in 1973 by a Presidential Advisory Committee.[17] Whatever the validity of those considerations, it is being recommended here for a different reason: from the standpoint of moral learning, plea bargaining clearly constitutes the single most destructive element of criminal justice in the United States.

Reducing Punitiveness and Cutting Expenditure

Enactment of the recommendations made thus far would bring us much closer to the ideal of every crime's being punished. But is the approximation feasible? Would it not make the system excessively punitive and expensive? Belief that it would has often been expressed. "If every policeman, every prosecutor, every court, and every post-sentence agency performed his or its responsibility in strict accordance with rules of law" claims Judge Breitel, "the criminal law would be ordered but intolerable. Living would be a sterile compliance with soul-killing rules and taboos. By comparison, a primitive tribal society would seem free."[18] There is some

109

merit to this claim: strict enforcement of our criminal statutes, overshot as they are,[19] would make the legal system intolerably punitive. Were we to respond by incarceration to every case of such crimes as pot smoking, drug abuse, prostitution, homosexual behavior, fornication, gambling, or various kinds of traffic violations, the hardship would be immense, and so many of us would end up in prison that the whole social system might collapse; and were we to convict all juveniles for conduct that is illegal only for children—for example, truancy, idleness, sleeping in alleys, running away from home, curfew violations, using vulgar language, begging, smoking, using alcohol, general "incorrigibility"—a very high proportion of all juveniles would end up in confinement. Moreover, strict enforcement would make costs of administration of justice prohibitive. If, under the present statutes, every criminal act were to be charged, and every charge "were subjected to a full-scale trial, the States and the Federal Government would need to multiply by many times the number of judges . . . , court facilities,"[20] prosecutors, public defenders, prison personnel, and space, and even then, the overburdening of the system could cause endless delays in processing cases.[21] On the other hand, in want of a vast investment of financial and human resources, strict enforcement policy would totally destroy the criminal process—merely the removal of plea bargaining could, in Judge Lummus's words, "break down the administration of criminal justice in any state in the Union."[22] Thus, approaching certainty of punishment must be accompanied by further changes in the criminal justice system—changes that would make the system less punitive and cut its costs.

The preceding comments imply how to make it less punitive. First, no behavior should ever be punished in violation of the dominant moral sentiment. Thus, crimes whose punishment runs against the sentiment should be removed from criminal codes—a recommendation that I made in a different context earlier and that must necessarily be implemented under the scrupulous enforcement proposed here. Homosexual behavior and drug abuse were used as instances of such behavior, and a few further items may be added to an actual or emerging list, for example, prostitution, extramarital sex, or attempted suicide.

Another recommendation refers to those among the *mala prohibita* where the moral sentiment of the society, being ambivalent, is not clearly antipunitive, but punishment is not universally demanded either. There are here such offenses as vagrancy, social gambling, drunkeness, or smoking marihuana, and all kinds of illegal juvenile acts that would not be crimes if committed by adults. Some of these *mala prohibita*—those where punishment does not serve any clearly useful social purpose—should be decriminalized, whereas thorough application of fines (or other mild penalties, such as restitution or performance of an act in the public interest) may become the best response to others. Decriminalization would include, in particular, acts illegal for juveniles only. Many of these acts fall within the normal process of growing up; many others are somewhat harmful, but only for the child himself; and some are just signals of impending danger. Thus, they often justify use of institutions for guidance and other community services but never of courts for juvenile delinquents.[23]

The two means—decriminalization and replacement of imprisonment by fines—would make systematic enforcement of punishments tolerable. Unwarranted penalties would disappear, and severe penalties would sanction genuine wrongdoing only. They would also cut costs; decriminalized crimes cost nothing, and fines constitute an economical penalty. Moreover, they would help decongest lower courts and thus make their badly needed reform easier.[24] Nevertheless, in view of the costs of systematic apprehending, trying, convicting, and confining nearly all genuine wrongdoers, these means would be clearly insufficient. They would have to be complemented by another—and by far the most effective—method of cost cutting. The method consists in simplifying the criminal procedure.

Recommendations of its simplifying abound (however, again, for reasons different from mine), and there are among their proponents such bodies as presidential commissions and task

IMPLICATIONS

forces,[25] the American Bar Association,[26] the American Law Institute,[27] and many others. The recommendations include, in particular, simplifying and tightening operations of the police by consolidation of police departments and by better police recruitment and training; broad use, in a way resembling many European systems, of orders of summary punishment in dealing with minor crimes (which would, again, help decongest lower courts); coordination of prosecutors' functions within each state; unification of state court systems under central administrations and technical improvement of court operations by use of modern management devices; simplification of pretrial proceedings by means such as removal of detention (unless screening of the suspect implies that, if undetained, he would flee, commit crimes, or hinder production of evidence), broader use of depositions, and expeditious filing and hearing of motions; restructuring of the review process to achieve prompt finality in appellate proceedings; and enactment of norms providing a single, swift postconviction remedy for infringements of constitutional rights.

Many of these recommendations are obviously correct, and some of them have already been adopted by a number of states or by federal law. However, their validity is common knowledge today, and therefore nothing would be gained by analyzing them here in detail. Instead, I focus on two changes that are important and controversial. One of them is a reconsideration of the jury system, and I shall discuss it briefly now. The other one—stimulation of confessions by means other than plea bargaining—is even more essential for acquisition of evidence than as a cost-cutting formula; that is why I shall discuss it in the next chapter, when dealing with evidence.

There is no doubt that abolition of the jury would greatly diminish expenditure. According to a 10-year-old estimate, the cost of an average New York jury trial exceeded $750 a day,[28] and a median jury trial takes about four days.[29] In pursuit of the ideal of punitive certainty, and especially in absence of plea bargaining, the total costs of the jury trials may increase dramatically—as I

112

said earlier, the very necessity of preventing this increase had become a major factor in the spread of negotiated pleas. Thus, abolition of the jury (or at least a far-going limitation of its use and size) may be considered a somewhat obvious cost-cutting device.

The device has been recommended not only for economic but also, and mainly, for substantial reasons. The jury has long been denounced, in this country and abroad, for a number of sins, the worst being its incompetence. Jurors are often accused of inability to understand the case they are deciding, to understand "what the judge tells them about the legal rules," [30] and to understand the weight and direction of the evidence. "The subtraction of relatively intelligent classes from the jury means that it is an understatement to describe a jury . . . as a group of twelve people of average intelligence." [31] In Dean Griswold's words, "the jury trial at best is the apotheosis of the amateur." [32] Owing to lack of understanding and, moreover, owing to bias, decisions of the jury often fail to follow the law: they are "capricious and arbitrary," [33] and they sometimes remit the due penalty as if the jurors had been vested the pardoning power.

Supporters of the jury respond to the criticism by a number of arguments. First, in any society, the value of the jury depends largely on the quality of the judiciary, and they question its quality in the United States. Judges are often open to prejudice and to outside influence, especially to political pressure and to favors. That is why the jury is a guarantor of integrity and an "inestimable safeguard . . . against the compliant, biased, or eccentric judge." [34] (To be sure, this role could hardly be fulfilled if jurors were as incompetent as their critics claim. However, the claim has been refuted by Kalven and Zeisel: their monumental study makes it clear that, for all practical purposes, the jury understands the case and its verdicts follow evidence. [35]) Furthermore, being, in their supporters' view, a representative cross-section of the community, juries operate as "instruments of public justice": [36] they ensure that court decisions match the country's moral sentiment. It is in this sense that Lord Devlin conceives each jury as a "little

113

parliament."[37] True, this "parliamentary" function may occasionally result in a court decision contrary to a particular norm of criminal law, if the norm is basically unjust or turns unjust when applied to the individual circumstances of an exceptional case. However, such conflicts between law and justice are rare, and when they sometimes occur, justice should prevail. Its supporters also claim that the jury, having been with us for so long, is cherished by litigants and by the general public. "We believe that trial by jury in criminal cases is fundamental to the American scheme of justice,"[38] and this very belief increases respect for and trust in criminal courts and their decisions.

This very incomplete list of arguments for and against has not been presented here to accept or legitimize an unconditional recommendation on whether the jury should stay with us as it is, disappear, or change; a recommendation of this kind would require an analysis exceeding by far the limits of this book. The arguments were referred to only to show how powerful—whatever the weight of the counterarguments—the reasons are for preservation of the jury, especially from the viewpoint of this study, with its stress on justice of punishments and prestige of courts. In spite of these reasons, however, a conditional recommendation against the jury seems to deserve approval: if further use of plea bargaining is a necessary price for preservation of juries, it would be better to abolish them than to continue the practice of plea negotiations. This is so since without negotiated pleas and without juries we would still be able to provide each accused with reasonably fair, though less than perfect, justice. On the other hand, under the present conditions, we deliver as perfect a justice as possible to approximately 5 percent of the accused, and a system of injustice, inconsistency, and uncertainty to the overwhelming majority of them.

What all this implies is an option: having abolished plea bargaining, we may either increase the expenditure for more numerous jury trials or rely on bench trials only. Accepting the latter should be made dependent on marked improvement of judicial standards. Accepting the former depends on the general will to invest new funds and human resources. However, the investment may be lower than assumed by defenders of plea bargaining.[39] The investment may be considerably reduced by a simple means: eliciting confessions without negotiations. Since, however, the means is essential not only for cost cutting but also, and mainly, for acquisition of evidence, I shall discuss it in the following chapter.

Chapter Six

PROVING THE TRUTH: CONFESSIONS

THE EVIDENTIAL ADVANTAGES of confessions have been discussed earlier: a confession is often necessary to acquire further evidence; it then constitutes a prerequisite for conviction of the guilty. The economic advantages of confession are clear: a confession during interrogation, if corroborated, results, at arraignment, in a plea of guilty, and, like any guilty plea, cuts expenditure and reduces workload. These double benefits justify a reconsideration of the constraints imposed by the *Miranda* (and *Escobedo*) constitutional construction. The reconsideration consists of making the values that underlie the constraints explicit, balancing them against the benefits brought about by confessions, and, finally, discovering alternative means to protect those values that count most and may not be abandoned.

117

IMPLICATIONS

The Underlying Values That Deserve Protection

Various court decisions, including *Miranda,* and numerous writings have clarified the values that the self-incrimination clause of the fifth amendment is supposed to protect. Some commentators view the privilege against self-incrimination as a moral axiom. From this perspective the privilege is itself a "fundamental value" on a par with such ultimate values as "liberty, and . . . man's immortal soul."[1] This view is not logically absurd, but the majority rightly opts for a utilitarian stand—the privilege exists, not for its own sake, but to protect a number of other values. The number, sometimes developed into a lengthy catalogue,[2] may be reduced to a few basic items: protecting the innocent, ensuring procedural fairness, maintaining equality, and protecting society from unjust law.

Protecting the innocent is an obvious and essential demand that no open society should compromise. Therefore, the risk of the guilty's going free is preferred in America over the risk of convicting the innocent. Coerced confession endangers the innocent, because it is unreliable, and even a requirement of corroborating evidence does not always entirely eliminate the danger. Thus, if the *Miranda* construction was necessary for its elimination, one would have to accept the construction even at the expense of punitive certainty and consistency.

Procedural fairness is another underlying value of importance. *Miranda* was meant to implement the due process requirement that it is better to let the guilty go free than to convict them by use of unfair means. With respect to the questioning of suspects, however, this is a vague proposition and may be neither accepted nor rejected until a determination is made of how much pressure would make an interrogation unfair. The determination requires a decision dependent on the moral feelings of the society at large. Thus, the Supreme Court, as "the keeper of the country's conscience,"[3] draws the demarcation line between the fair and the unfair means of questioning suspects.

118

In recent decades the Court has pushed the line outward to hold an expanding number of questioning techniques unfair. American courts have always denounced torture and other outright physical violence. Moreover, since the 1940s the Supreme Court has held various kinds of psychological pressure unfair. For example, it held confessions unfair that resulted from questioning the suspect for 36 hours without respite, sleep, or rest,[4] pointing loaded guns against the suspect's head while asking him incriminating questions,[5] and threatening to take a suspect's children from her if she did not cooperate.[6] These are ruthless practices, reminiscent of the Star Chamber inquisitorial procedure. The Court has, however, added various kinds of milder pressure to the list of unfair interrogation techniques. These techniques include expressing false sympathy, providing an air of confidence in the suspect's guilt, and using the "Mutt and Jeff" technique.[7] In addition, the Court has reversed convictions involving relatively minor deprivations. These include failure to provide food during eight hours of custody[8]; incommunicado detention of the suspect without an opportunity to contact spouse, friend, or attorney[9]; displeasure and tension due to "unfamiliar surroundings" at the police station[10]; loss of privacy resulting from interrogation;[11] and inequality between the suspect and his interrogators.[12] Thus, the Court has construed "unfair means" very broadly, encompassing even mild and unintentional pressures that are inherent in any interrogation.

Unfortunately, the proper demarcation line between fair and unfair means of interrogating suspects cannot be precisely delineated. What is fair in the legal process depends on the moral views of the society at large as perceived by the Court. The moral views of any society tend to adjust intuitively to its needs. People tend to appraise behavior useful for the social group as intrinsically good and socially harmful behavior as intrinsically wrong.[13] The needs of the group change in the course of its development, and the appraisals change to correspond. The same behavior may be functional, and thus perceived as right, on a low level of social de-

IMPLICATIONS

velopment but may become dysfunctional, and perceived as wrong, on a higher level. This principle holds true, in particular, with appraisals of court and police behavior in the criminal process. Thus, in an almost crime-free social group the uppermost standards for both courts and police may be functional. On the other hand, high standards may prove harmful in a crime-ridden society in which punitive certainty is badly needed, and thus they have to be compromised. How much compromise is needed depends in particular on the extent of criminality. In the United States there apparently is no need, and no general demand, to compromise judicial standards. The behavior of judges must therefore be impeccable. Police, on the other hand, are expected to display a more mundane level of perfection.

This principle provides some guidance for drawing a demarcation line between fair and unfair means of interrogation. Most people in this country would consider physical or mental torture unfair. On the other hand, many relatively innocent police tactics, such as false sympathy or the "Mutt and Jeff" technique, do not seem to invite general contempt, especially when applied to solve a major crime. Apparently, the same holds true with incommunicado detention for a limited period of time, discomfort, and loss of privacy in interrogation. Of course, the extent to which the tactics or the detention is acceptable depends partly on the suspect. For suspects who are weak or sick, otherwise mild tactics or detention may indeed amount to the "torture of mind." [14] Nor does the majority demand equality between the police and the suspect. The very fact of arrest and interrogation suggests police power over the suspect, with the resulting inequality of roles. The only legitimate concern is that the power not be abused; the power of the police over the accused must neither lead to conviction of the innocent nor be applied unfairly. However, the very exercise of this power, which is intrinsic to the interrogation, cannot reasonably be considered as unfair. In sum, although extreme pressure on a suspect deserves disapproval, a reasonable degree of pressure does not infringe procedural fairness.

120

Equal protection is another value underlying *Miranda*. Some commentators[15] argue that wealthy and professional criminals are well aware that they cannot be made to speak and therefore will say nothing until counsel arrives. The poor and the ignorant, on the other hand, are unaware of their right to remain silent and are particularly likely to succumb. Thus, to achieve equality, the police must give warnings "designed to lead the indigent and the ignorant to behave as do the wealthy and the knowledgeable."[16] Whatever the value of the principle of equal justice, the argument contains a double fallacy. First, its premises are partly false. Not only the indigent and the ignorant, but also the wealthy and the educated, have often been unaware that they can refuse to respond to interrogation.[17] Second, and more importantly, its conclusion is a non sequitur. The equal protection clause must not be extended blindly and harmfully. The clause does not demand that, because some murderers and rapists are, unfortunately, smart enough to cripple interrogation and avoid punishment, we should make all others equally smart. In the well-known words of Chief Justice Weintraub:

The Constitution is not at all offended when a guilty man stubs his toe. On the contrary, it is decent to hope that he will. . . . [A]s to the culprit who reveals his guilt unwittingly with no intent to shed his inner burden, it is no more unfair to use the evidence he thereby reveals than it is to turn against him clues at the scene of the crime which a brighter, better informed, or more gifted criminal would not have left. . . . It is consonant with good morals, and the Constitution, to exploit a criminal's ignorance or stupidity in the detectional process.[18]

The last important value underlying *Miranda* is protecting men from laws that are unjust, that is, unsupported by the moral views of the society. In any society some tension exists between law and morality. The tension is especially evident in oppressive systems. Even in democracies, however, some discrepancies emerge for several reasons. As I said earlier, the moral views of any society evolve continually, while legal norms become easily

121

fixed and difficult to change. Moreover, the process of checking lawmakers sometimes fails, resulting in the enactment of morally dubious norms. The impact of grave social problems may cause democratic processes to deteriorate temporarily, resulting in bad laws and abusive legal practices. Furthermore, because legal norms are articulated in an abstract manner, they may appear unjust when applied to an exceptional case. In any of these events the danger of a morally unfounded conviction occurs, and thus the search for procedural shelters begins. The privilege against self-incrimination is one shelter, and if viewed from this perspective, the *Miranda* requirements enhance the shelter immensely. The warnings inhibit unjust conviction by instructing the suspect on how to cripple criminal law enforcement in general. Of course, if this was the main value underlying *Miranda,* it might hardly be accepted in the United States. In open societies relatively few norms of criminal law are unjust. Consequently, impairment of the whole criminal justice system to prevent an exceptional bad norm from working would be absurd. Thus, only reasonable safeguards against bad norms are needed.[19]

In sum, three of the *Miranda* values—protection against bad laws, egalitarianism, and excessive fairness—do not outweigh the benefits brought by confessions. Only protection of the innocent and reasonable procedural fairness are of utmost importance and must be kept safe.

The Construction to Fit the Values

The values of protecting the innocent and providing reasonable procedural fairness may be preserved by means other than the *Miranda* warnings. The Warren Court was clearly aware of it:

It is impossible for us to foresee the potential alternatives . . . . Therefore we cannot say that the Constitution necessarily requires adherence to any particular solution for . . . compulsions of the interrogation process . . . . We encourage Congress and the States to continue their laudable

122

search for increasingly effective ways of protecting the rights of the individual while promoting efficient enforcement of our criminal laws. However, unless we are shown other procedures which are at least as effective in apprising accused persons of their right of silence and in assuring a continuous opportunity to exercise it, the [*Miranda*] . . . safeguards must be observed.[20]

The passage seems to go too far when pronouncing the suspect's constitutional right to silence and its corollaries—an issue to which I shall return soon. Nevertheless, the basic notion that alternative, legislative means may better both prevent police abuse and promote efficient law enforcement is correct. Pleas for legislative action to prevent the abuse had long preceded *Miranda*.[21] However, "[p]erhaps because constitutional doctrines did not then . . . threaten the extinction of police questioning, the proposals met with public indifference or hostility"[22] and did not result in the intended statutory change. When facing the continuing abuse, the Warren Court was, of course, unable to provide comprehensive legislation. Thus, the only remedy at its disposal was the pronouncement of a sweeping exclusionary rule. There seemed to be an implicit alternative speculation by the *Miranda* majority. If the new exclusionary rule prevents police abuse without harming law enforcement, a clear advantage will result. On the other hand, if the exclusionary rule harms law enforcement, it would provoke legislative implementation of alternative remedies to make the reversal of *Miranda* constitutionally feasible and thereby yield another favorable solution.

The other favorable solution is evidently needed, and the preceding analysis determines its shape. Because the two basic values—protecting the innocent and providing reasonable procedural fairness—are endangered primarily by the invisibility of police interrogation, a supervision of the interrogation process is necessary.[23] Thus, the state legislatures, with federal aid and assistance,[24] must implement supervision and select specific means for checking the police. A number of supervision techniques are available.[25] A combination of using electronic devices and judicial supervision seems to be optimal. The first technique consists of mandatory sound or visual recordings of all police station interrogation rooms.[26] This practice could be supplemented by frequent and unexpected visits by specially trained judicial officers[27] to interrogation rooms. Exclusive control of the recording devices would reside with judicial officers rather than with the police.[28] This combination of techniques would provide a comprehensive check of police station interrogations. Moreover, the judicial officers could interview at random a considerable proportion of suspects and police officers concerning the course of any preceding field questioning to uncover possible police abuse outside of the station house.[29] In addition, an improved system of sanctioning police misconduct could be implemented. The traditional means, especially tort, criminal, and internal disciplinary liability, are inadequate.[30] Thus, new remedies, such as contempt of court proceedings or civilian review board disciplinary sanctions, deserve consideration.[31]

Once the states introduce effective means of checking police interrogation, the *Miranda* warnings will become unnecessary, provided the innovations withstand constitutional scrutiny. New methods of interrogation control will allow the Court to overrule *Miranda* and apply the privilege against self-incrimination, as it had been prior to *Miranda,* from the time of arraignment only. With *Miranda* overruled, numerous state statutes that were promulgated to implement the *Miranda* requirements would probably soon be repealed. Of course, the overruling of *Miranda* and the repeal of the state statutes would not amount to the introduction of the suspect's duty to talk to interrogators. Because everyone is free to act in any manner not proscribed by the law, the suspect would be free to talk or not to talk. Thus, the suspect's freedom to be silent, which results from the silence of the law and not from a pronounced legal privilege, would not necessitate any claim for warnings.

Effective supervision of interrogations would also remove

the need for a lawyer to be present at the interrogation. Under *Escobedo* and *Miranda* the lawyer must play a double role. First, when conferring with the suspect in private, he is to advise the suspect of the right to silence. Second, merely by observing police behavior in the interrogation room, he is to prevent police abuse, and if abuse still occurs, to confront the prosecution with it at trial. Thus, the lawyer must both advise his client and effectuate *Miranda*. If the *Miranda* requirements are abandoned and substituted by well-supervised interrogations, the lawyer's double function will become unnecessary.[32] Consequently, the overruling of both *Miranda* and *Escobedo* will become reasonable and thus limit the constitutional right to counsel to postarraignment procedures.

If both decisions are overruled, the due process clause would again control prearraignment interrogation. A full return to the "voluntariness-totality of circumstances" era, however, will not be required, because the new supervision techniques will eliminate the secrecy of interrogation and the consequent poor chance of proving police abuse. On the other hand, the Court will again face the problem of distinguishing between a fair and an unfair amount of pressure used against a suspect. A demarcation line was suggested earlier, with physical and mental torture on one side and minor police tactics on the other.[33] Clearly, one kind of effective pressure should be not only located on the legitimate side of the line but encouraged: making the nonresponsive suspect know that his silence might be commented upon at trial—not as a sufficient proof of guilt, of course, but as a fact that the court might take into account when weighing the evidence.

It is true that the demarcation line is far from precise, but there is no easy answer to this definitional problem. The borderline tactics would have to be reviewed on a case-by-case basis, and the decisions will depend on the judicial perception of both the moral views of society and the basic social needs to be served by criminal justice. This process will require the courts to make subtle definitions and distinctions about borderline practices and thus will

125

Chapter Seven

HUMANITARIANISM RECONSIDERED

Criticism of the Recommendations

IN THE PRECEDING chapters a number of changes have been recommended. Their acceptance would bring us closer to the state where a just punishment follows every crime committed. This would, in turn, bring, through the process of moral learning, a sweeping decline in criminal behavior, and, consequently, alleviation of the crime-engendered social ills. Still, a difficult question arises: is the ideal of just and certain punishment humane?

Its price, especially in terms of human suffering, is high, and a critic could argue against it forcefully. The following criticism might be offered. The approximation to the ideal means that the overwhelming majority of criminals would be incarcerated, and the consequences, even if beneficial for the rest of us, would be disastrous for them. Under the present system the overwhelming majority of crime perpetrators avoid incarceration. Having avoided it, they then, more often than not, abandon criminal behavior. Many of them have been just occasional lawbreakers; many others renounce crime owing to maturation or to a variety of helpful social influences that operate outside of penal institutions. On the other hand, once incarcerated, they easily become hopeless cases, and under the system close to full enforcement, large numbers of them would get incarcerated.

The reason for the hopelessness may be easily spelled out by the critic. It consists in the demoralizing influence of confinement. Prisons corrupt the inmates. The corruption occurs, in particular, because of the physical conditions of prison life, abuse and cruelty on the part of other convicts, isolation from outside influences, and, especially, prolonged association with other lawbreakers from whom the inmate learns criminal attitudes and techniques. Moreover, according to a widespread belief, the stigma of being labeled a criminal and incarcerated helps build a criminal self-image and thus itself becomes a criminogenic influence. It also begets, in the society at large, reactions that, after release, hamper adjustment to the noncriminal world.

All this is considered as particularly true with respect to juvenile delinquents. They are more susceptible than adults to any learning process, right or wrong, and therefore they get more easily demoralized in the company of their delinquent and criminal inmates. Being less mature, they are more open to the criminogenic impact of the labeling and stigma.

Thus, implementing changes proposed in this book would wreck the lives of a large proportion of lawbreakers. This is a merciless policy. Lawbreakers are as human as anyone and suffer more. Therefore, they deserve compassion and help rather than destruction. The need for sympathy and help is most acute on the part of juvenile delinquents; they are on the border of childhood and are not always fully able to understand and control their behavior. That is why destroying their lives by prolonged incarceration is particularly cruel.

Countercriticism: Severity of Punishment, Stigma, Juveniles

However convincing this criticism may appear, a substantial part of it should be qualified. First, the harshness of incarceration should not be overstated under the proposals presented earlier. To be sure, periods of confinement must be long enough to implement the process of instrumental learning, and their length must increase with the growing harmfulness of crimes and with the growing guilt of wrongdoers. This does not amount, however, to a general recommendation of very severe penalties. There is a strong temptation, on the part of those who consider general deterrence as the basic function of criminal law, to make punishment very severe: rising severity increases deterrence, and even an occasional punishment, if extremely harsh, may arouse, in some potential wrongdoers, a fear strong enough to effectively deter them once and for all.[1] If deterrence were the main function of criminal law, this would be a legitimate stand. But the replacement of deterrence by moral education makes the stand fallacious: an excessively harsh punishment is unjust and, therefore, not only void of persuasive moral power but counterproductive.[2] To become an effective implement of moral learning, criminal punishment must be of a just severity: its measure, as well as its kind, must match the dominant feeling of justice.

It is true that conditions in penal institutions can hardly be made congenial for unmaking the criminal or even averting his corruption in confinement; in particular, there is no easy way to prevent his associating with and learning from fellow wrongdoers. However, the brutalizing physical conditions, overcrowding, humiliation, and cruelties can and should be prevented. Moreover, education and professional training to improve his chances after release deserve new stress, and so does voluntary psychological counseling, which should be applied not so much to treat him—the philosophy of large-scale rehabilitation is illusory—as to help in alleviating the pain of being confined.

IMPLICATIONS

It is also true that the very stigma of being convicted may make the convict's future adjustment difficult. The difficulties are, however, less significant than widely believed and are outbalanced by benefits of stigmatizing wrongdoers. Those who overemphasize the difficulties—a group of criminologists who profess a loose set of ideas known as the "labeling perspective"—make two claims on this issue, the first being that hostility and mistrust of general society often hamper the convict's adjustment after his release. This is obviously true; however, the harm should be prevented by a well-arranged system of postrelease remedies rather than by leaving criminals unpunished. Second, and more importantly, they claim that the criminal self-image aroused by the stigma is itself criminogenic. When one or a few occasional deviant acts are encountered by penalties and stigma is imposed on the perpetrator, the encounter brings about "strengthening of the deviant conduct as a negative reaction to the stigmatizing . . . and ultimate acceptance of deviant social status."[3] Thus, being labeled a deviant changes one's self-perception and leads to the emergence of an increasing commitment to deviance. The claim, in spite of its wide appeal among sociologists and much of the general public, is unwarranted: it is gratuitous and imprecise and would prove false if referred to criminal behavior and made specific enough to be tested. It is gratuitous, because it finds no support in psychology—there is no known psychological process that would lead from stigmatizing the wrongdoer to his permanent attachment to wrongdoing.[4] Its lack of precision is, in particular, due to its focus on "deviance"—a term that is almost meaninglessly vague.[5] If specified and referred to some noncriminal behavior or conditions, the claim is valid. For instance, a child labeled at school as unable may easily lose faith in his ability, stop learning, and eventually lose whatever ability he has had.[6] Or a man labeled impotent may, because of anxiety aroused by the label, become sexually handicapped. However, no similar process operates within those stigmatized as murderers, robbers, thieves, or rapists. Although the assertion criticized here had been made almost thirty years ago[7] and then had found a large number of supporters,[8] it has never been corroborated with respect to criminal behavior.

No wonder. From the viewpoint outlined in the first part of this book, not only is the assertion fallacious, but also, in a way, its opposite is true. Stigmatizing criminals by courts and by the society at large is an essential component of persuasive communications—one of the two mechanisms by which all of us, especially potential lawbreakers, acquire moral evaluations. Thus, the stigmatizing does not foster wrongdoing: by "putting the guilty on the *index,* holding him at a distance, ostracizing him,"[9] the stigma prevents criminal behavior. This adaptive role implies that it should be encouraged, not undermined. From 'this stand, the claim of criminogenic character of stigma is not only untrue but harmful. Wide dissemination of the false contention that we who condemn the criminals cause wrongdoing rather than the criminals themselves undermines the adaptive process of condemning them. Its undermining is one more reason why we can see, with increasing frequency, on television screens and elsewhere, apprehended wrongdoers who, instead of hiding their faces, look and smile shamelessly. They learned the lesson: the viewers, and not they, are guilty. Worse than that, the lesson is being learned by an increasing proportion of viewers.

Compassion for children is another ground for the criticism. Indeed, if certainty of punishment for juvenile delinquents were achieved under the otherwise unchanged criminal laws of this country, the majority of adolescents would end up in confinement. One major reason for this is that there is much conduct illegal for juveniles only; another reason consists in overshooting by those criminal norms that are addressed to adults and juveniles alike. However, my recommendations imply both limiting juvenile delinquency to acts that would be criminal if committed by adults and removing unwarranted adult penalties from criminal codes. These changes would alleviate the excessive impact of the increased punitive certainty on adolescents.

To be sure, the impact would still be harsh. Approximation

131

IMPLICATIONS

of punitive certainty would be quickly followed by confinement of a much higher proportion of juveniles than is the case under the present system. This is, however, exactly what is badly needed. The same process of persuasive instrumental learning outlined in the first part of this book operates in both adults and juveniles. Thus, the prerequisities for its effectiveness are identical for both groups. This does not mean, of course, that courts, procedure, kind of confinement, and amount of punishment should necessarily be identical. Nor does it mean that children who, because of immaturity, are unable to understand or control their behavior should be punished. It only implies that certainty of punishment, as well as its justice, constitutes the basic prerequisite of vicarious moral learning, not only by adults, but also by adolescents.

Conclusion

Thus, the above criticism of my recommendations is exaggerated. On the other hand, the price of suffering to be paid for a system of just and certain punishments is high. It consists in confinement of a population, adult and juvenile, much larger than the total inmate population of today and, consequently, in inflicting much more pain and wrecking many more lives than under the present system.

However, the hardship will affect only the "first generation" of criminals—those who would commit crimes in the period immediately following the introduction of the recommended changes. Their just and certain punishment will stimulate the process of persuasive instrumental learning that, in turn, will bring about extensive decline of criminal behavior. Furthermore, even their number may be limited by an advance promulgation of the recommended changes; some of them would simply be deterred from breaking the (since then relentless) law.

Humanitarians, especially those of the utilitarian persuasion, consider minimizing total human suffering as an ultimate value. Humanitarians dealing with criminal justice are inclined to focus on total suffering of one group only: the criminal law-breakers. Even with the interest limited to the actual and potential lawbreakers, however, the foregoing recommendations meet the humanitarian demand. Soon after their introduction the total sum of suffering of the lawbreakers would clearly decline. This would be so, since life committed to crime is essentially miserable. Owing to the implementation of these proposals, the overwhelming majority of potential lawbreakers will, following the just and certain punishment of the "first generation," forego the criminal way and avoid the misery. Thus, even from this very limited humanitarian perspective, the recommendations appear to be worthwhile.

Needless to say, they seem even more useful from the standpoint of humanitarianism's covering, as it should, the whole of society. By preventing crime, they would avert the suffering of its victims, the suffering of all those paralyzed by fear of crime, and the suffering due to the many broader social ills that are generated or intensified by the pervasiveness of criminal behavior. Accepting the recommendations would, in a manner not irrelevant to humanitarian concerns, eventually bring about a general improvement of the social fabric and, by making men better, contribute to the moral progress of our society.

Notes

Introduction

1. FBI, *Uniform Crime Reports 1975*, U.S. Department of Justice, Washington, D.C., 1976, p. 49, Table 2 and *Uniform Crime Reports 1977*, U.S. Department of Justice, Washington, D.C. 1978, p. 37, Table 2).

2. This is a conclusion from victimization survey statistics, *cf. Sourcebook of Criminal Justice Statistics 1975*, U.S. Department of Justice, Law Enforcement Assistance Administration, 1976, p. 338, Table 3.1.

3. FBI, *Uniform Crime Reports 1975*, pp. 26, 28, 31.

4. National Criminal Justice Information and Statistics Service, *Expenditure and Employment Data for the Criminal Justice System 1974*, U.S. Government Printing Office, Washington, D.C. 1976, p. 21, Table 2.

5. "The Losing Battle Against Crime in America," *U.S. News and World Report*, December 16, 1974, pp. 30–40, 32.

6. James Q. Wilson, *Thinking About Crime*, New York: Basic Books, 1975, p. 21.

7. John E. Conklin, *The Impact of Crime*, New York: Macmillan Publishing Co., 1975, p. 8.

8. President's Commission on Law Enforcement and Administration of Justice, *The Chal-*

135

INTRODUCTION

lenge of Crime in a Free Society, Washington, D.C., U.S. Government Printing Office, 1967, p. 49.

9. Goethe, *Faust,* Part 1, 1995–96.

Chapter One: Learning

1. The notions of counteraction and provocation, as well as distinctions made in the preceding paragraph, come from a modified version of Petrazycki's theory. (The modification consists, in particular, in the rejection of his unusual demarcation line between law and morality.) Cf. Leon Petrazycki, *Law and Morality,* Cambridge, Mass.: Harvard University Press, 1955, pp. 14, 31–62; Jan Gorecki, "Leon Petrazycki," in Jan Gorecki, ed., *Sociology and Jurisprudence of Leon Petrazycki,* Urbana, Ill.: University of Illinois Press, 1975, pp. 5–6.

2. Its peculiarly human character may be assumed but not asserted; phenomenologically similar experiences are not inconceivable among some animals, especially social insects, which display great self-sacrificial altruism. (For a review of both professional and literary observations on altruism of social insects, see Donald T. Campbell, "On the Conflicts between Biological and Social Evolution and between Psychology and Moral Tradition," 30 *American Psychologist* 1975, pp. 1113–14.)

3. Jerzy Lande, "The Sociology of Petrazycki," in Jan Gorecki, ed., *Sociology and Jurisprudence of Leon Petrazycki,* p. 34.

4. On the acceptance of evidently false factual statements due to opinions of fellow members of the group, see the famous experiment by Asch (Solomon E. Asch, "Effects of Group Pressure upon the Modification and Distortion of Judgment," in H. Guetzkow, ed., *Groups, Leadership and Men,* Pittsburgh: The Carnegie Press, 1951, pp. 177–90; Solomon E. Asch, *Social Psychology,* New York: Prentice-Hall, 1952, pp. 450–501), repeated by a number of follow-up studies.

5. Kenneth E. Anderson, *Persuasion Theory and Practice,* Boston, Mass.: Allyn and Bacon, 1971, pp. 234, 217–18.

6. Robert K. Merton, *Social Theory and Social Structure,* New York: Free Press, 1968, p. 357.

7. In Clyde Kluckhohn's words, "no culture forms survive unless they constitute responses which are adjustive or adaptive" (*Navaho Witchcraft,* XXII Papers of the Peabody Museum, Cambridge, Mass.: Peabody Museum, 1944, p. 46). For similar views see, e.g., Bronislaw Malinowski, "Anthropology," *Encyclopaedia Britannica,* 1926, Suppl. I, pp. 132–33.

8. Jerzy Lande, "The Sociology of Petrazycki," pp. 34–35.

9. Cf., e.g., the following "explanation" by Kluckhohn (*Navaho Witchcraft,* p. 47): "The at present mechanically useless buttons on the sleeve of a European man's suit subserve the 'function' of preserving the familiar, of maintaining a tradition. People are, in general, more comfortable if they feel a continuity of behavior, if they feel themselves as following out the orthodox and socially approved forms of behavior." For criticism of this and similar

1. LEARNING

explanatory trivia, cf., e.g., R. K. Merton, *Social Theory and Social Structure,* pp. 84–86, (from which Kluckhohn's words above are quoted); Carl G. Hempel, *Aspects of Scientific Explanation,* New York: The Free Press, 1965, p. 322; Maria Ossowska, *Social Determinants of Moral Ideas,* London: Routledge and Kegan Paul, 1971, p. 104.

10. To make their meaning more precise, I am construing "social needs" as relative to various specific attributes whose preservation constitutes the defining standard of a society's adaptation (which, broadly speaking, matches the methodological requirements of Ernest Nagel, "A Formalization of Functionalism," in *Logic Without Metaphysics,* Glencoe, Ill.: The Free Press, 1956, pp. 253 ff., and Carl G. Hempel, *Aspects of Scientific Explanation,* pp. 303–23). Even thus relativized, the "social needs" are, of course, less clear than the "vital needs of an organism" used in functional biological explanations: "in regard to the condition of survival by a society, there is nothing comparable in this domain to the generally acknowledged 'vital functions' of biology as defining attributes of living organisms" (Ernest Nagel, *The Structure of Science,* New York: Harcourt, Brace and World, Inc., 1961, p. 527). However imperfect, this understanding of "social needs" is at least specific enough for the following reconsideration of the functional approach to moral evaluations.

11. For the most comprehensive refutation of universal functionalism, see R. K. Merton, *Social Theory and Social Structure,* pp. 79–91.

12. The high degree of integration of illiterate societies explains why the idea of universal functionalism was developed primarily by social anthropologists (see on this R. K. Merton, *idem,* p. 82). However, since in illiterate societies there also operate counteracting factors other than plurality of groups (cf. the following text), and in particular a general ignorance and religious superstitions, dysfunctional evaluations often win the refferendum even in a primitive tribe.

13. Albert Bandura, *Principles of Behavior Modification,* New York: Holt, Rinehart and Winston, 1969, p. 25.

14. Cf. notes 20 and 21, *infra.*

15. On other benefits of vicarious learning see Albert Bandura, "Analysis of Modeling Processes," in Albert Bandura, ed., *Psychological Modeling,* Chicago: Aldine, 1971, p. 3.

16. By the "most advanced form" I mean awareness understood as verbal comprehension of correct contingencies of reinforcement or punishment. Some kind of nonverbal "comprehension" may be present among animals and especially among primates, as claimed by Gestalt psychologists (cf., in particular, W. Kohler, *The Mentality of Apes,* New York: Harcourt-Brace, 1925. For an excellent summary of critical appraisals of Kohler's and related views, see D. E. Berlyne, *Structure and Direction in Thinking,* New York: John Wiley & Sons, 1965, pp. 329–46). The rather vague issue of evolutionary emergence and advancement of symbolic capacities may be clarified and answered in a publicly convincing way by future progress in the biochemistry of our nervous system. As one optimistic theorist of thinking claims, "there must be psychological, physiological, and ultimately physicochemical laws whose action is manifest throughout the spectrum of behavior from the crudest to the loftiest. *We shall, no doubt, eventually understand* how a nervous system evolving in certain directions must sooner or later reach a level at which symbolic capacities come into existence, and how symbolic capacities, having advanced to a particular stage, must give rise to thinking." (D. E. Berlyne, *idem,* p. 6, emphasis added)

1. LEARNING

17. The amount of empirical evidence that corroborates this view (and thus refutes the purely cognitive perception of instrumental learning) is abundant (cf., e.g., D. B. Philbrick and L. Postman, "A Further Analysis of 'Learning Without Awareness,' " 68 *American J. of Psychology*, 1955, 417–24; J. Hirsch, "Learning Without Awareness and Extinction Following Awareness as a Function of Reinforcement," 54 *J. of Experimental Psychology*, 1957, 218–24; L. Postman and J. Sassenrath, "The Automatic Action of Verbal Rewards and Punishments," 65 *J. of General Psychology*, 1961, 109–36; J. M. Sassenrath, "Transfer of Learning Without Awareness," 10 *Psychological Reports*, 1962, 411–20; F. Thaver and W. F. Oakes, "Generalization and Awareness in Verbal Operant Conditioning," 6 *J. of Personality and Social Psychology*, 1967, 391–9; Thomas D. Kennedy, "Verbal Conditioning Without Awareness," 84 *J. of Experimental Psychology*, 1970, 487–94; Maj-Britt Lindahl, "Awareness, Conditioning, and Information Processing in Complex Learning Situations," 14 *Scandinavian J. of Psychology*, 1973, 121–30.

18. Albert Bandura, *Principles of Behavior Modification*, p. 569.

19. It is not quite clear whether empathetic elicitation results predominantly from intuiting emotions of the model or from imaginal representation of rewarding or noxious effects occurring to the observer himself (cf. Ezra Stotland, "Explanatory Investigations of Empathy," in L. Berkowitz, ed., *Advances in Experimental Social Psychology*, vol. 4, New York: Academic Press 1969, pp. 288–97).

20. High effectiveness of conditioning through vicarious emotional arousal by live or filmed models has been analyzed and corroborated by a large number of studies, e.g.: Seymour M. Berger, "Conditioning Through Vicarious Instigation," 69 *Psychological Review*, 1962, 450–66; Richard W. Walters, Marion Leat, and Louis Mezei, "Inhibition and Disinhibition of Responses through Empathetic Learning," 17 *Canadian Journal of Psychology*, 1963, 235–43; A. Bandura and T. L. Rosenthal, "Vicarious Classical Conditioning as a Function of Arousal Level," 3 *Journal of Personality and Social Psychology*, 1966, 54–62; R. D. O'Connor, "Modification of Social Withdrawal Through Symbolic Modeling," 2 *Journal of Applied Behavioral Analysis*, 1969, 15–22; Robert M. Liebert and Luis E. Fernandez, "Effects of Vicarious Consequences on Imitative Performance," 41 *Child Development*, 1970, 847–52; G. A. Marlatt, "A Comparison of Vicarious and Direct Reinforcement Control of Verbal Behavior in an Interview Setting," 16 *J. of Personality and Social Psychology*, 1970, 695–703 (with evidence that, under certain conditions, vicarious reinforcement does produce greater effects than direct reinforcement). On a related problem—vicarious extinction of previously learned aversion—see the seminal investigations by Bandura and his associates, especially: A. Bandura, J. Grusec, and F. L. Menlove, "Vicarious Extinction of Avoidance Behavior," 5 *J. of Personality and Social Psychology*, 1967, 16–23; A. Bandura and F. L. Menlove, "Factors Determining Vicarious Extinction of Avoidance Behavior Through Symbolic Modeling," 8 *J. of Personality and Social Psychology*, 1968, 99–108; A. Bandura, E. B. Blanchard, and B. Ritter, "Relative Efficacy of Desensitization and Modeling Approaches for Inducing Behavioral, Affective, and Attitudinal Changes," 13 *J. of Personality and Social Psychology*, 1969, 173–99; cf. also a critical survey of a number of studies by S. Rachman, "Clinical Applications of Observational Learning, Imitation and Modeling," 3 *Behavior Therapy*, 1972, 379–97, and a recent report on a practical application by Barbara G. Melamed and Lawrence J. Siegel, "Reduction of Anxiety in Children

Facing Hospitalization and Surgery by Use of Filmed Modeling," 43 *J. of Consulting and Clinical Psychology*, 1975, 511–21.

21. The fact that verbally evoked images are capable of producing attractive or aversive emotional effects has been well documented by numerous studies dealing with direct stimulation (e.g., Theodore Xenophon Barber and Karl W. Hahn, "Experimental Studies in 'Hypnotic' Behavior: Physiologic and Subjective Effects of Imaginal Pain," 139 *J. of Nervous and Mental Disease*, 1964, 416–25; William W. Grings, "Verbal-Perceptual Factors in the Conditioning of Autonomic Responses," in William F. Prokasy, ed., *Classical Conditioning: A Symposium*, New York: Appleton, 1965, pp. 71–89; S. S. Anant, "A Note on the Treatment of Alcoholics by a Verbal Aversion Technique," 8 *Canadian Psychologist*, 1967, 19–22; Michael E. Dawson and William W. Grings, "Comparison of Classical Conditioning and Relational Learning," 76 *J. of Experimental Psychology*, 1968, 227–31) and, most importantly for this writing, with vicarious stimulation (e.g., J. R. Cautela, "Covert Modeling," paper presented at 5th Annual Meeting of the Association for the Advancement of Behavior Therapy, Washington D. C., September 1971; J. R. Cautela, R. Flannery and E. Hanley, "Covert Modeling: An Experimental Test," 5 *Behavior Therapy*, 1974, 494–502; Alan E. Kazdin, "Covert Modeling and the Reduction of Avoidance Behavior," 81 *J. of Abnormal Psychology*, 1973, 87–95; cf. also Albert Bandura, "Modeling Theory," in W. S. Sahakian, ed., *Psychology of Learning: Systems, Models and Theories*, Chicago: Markham, 1970, 350–67, at 360–361).

22. Ross D. Parke, "The Role of Punishment in the Socialization Process," in Ronald A. Hoppe, G. Alexander Milton, and Edward S. Simmel, eds., *Early Experiences in the Process of Socialization*, New York: Academic Press, 1970, pp. 86–87.

23. Cf. K. E. Renner, "Delay of Reinforcement: A Historical Review," 61 *Psychological Bulletin*, 1964, 341–61; see Atkinson's experiment referred to in E. R. Hilgard, R. C. Atkinson and R. L. Atkinson, *Introduction to Psychology*, New York: Harcourt-Brace-Jovanovich, 1971, p. 206.

24. Cf., e.g., N. E. Miller, "Learning of Visceral and Glandular Responses," 163 *Science*, 1969, 434–45.

25. Cf. experiments referred to by Ross D. Parke, "The Role of Punishment," p. 84.

26. "[T]here is every reason to expect from informal observation that, in the case of humans, symbolic activities can effectively mediate a delayed reinforcement contingency without any appreciable loss of behavioral control. Therefore, if contingencies are explicitly defined for an individual he is able to link eventual consequences with particular performances." (Albert Bandura, *Principles of Behavior Modification*, p. 231); on the impact of awareness on effectiveness of delayed punishment, cf. R. D. Parke, ed., *Recent Trends in Social Learning Theory*, New York: Academic Press, 1972, pp. 86–87.

27. The distinction between variable and fixed schedules of intermittent reinforcement is well established in psychology of learning: winning in gambling is an instance of the former, and periodical salary payment, of the latter.

28. This has been discovered by L. G. Humphreys ("The Effect of Random Alternation of Reinforcement on the Acquisition and Extinction of Conditioned Eyelid Reactions," 25 *J.*

1. LEARNING

of Experimental Psychology, 1939, 141–58; "Acquisition and Extinction of Verbal Expectations in a Situation Analogous to Conditioning," idem, pp. 294–301) and then reaffirmed in a variety of situations by other experimenters (cf. W. O. Jenkins and J. C. Stanley, "Partial Reinforcement: A Review and Critique," 47 Psychological Bulletin, 1950, 193–234).

29. Cf., e.g., Sheldon Glueck and Eleanor Glueck, Unraveling Juvenile Delinquency, Cambridge, Mass.: Harvard University Press, 1950, p. 131; William McCord, Joan McCord, and Irving Kenneth Zola, Origins of Crime, New York: Columbia University Press, 1959, pp. 76–79, 101–3, 154–55.

30. Cf. Robert R. Sears, Eleanor E. Maccoby and Harry Levin, Patterns of Child Rearing, White Plains, N.Y.: Row, Peterson, 1957, pp. 172–73.

31. For instance, by R. T. Brown and A. R. Wagner, "Resistance to Punishment and Extinction Following Training with Shock or Nonreinforcement," 68 J. of Experimental Psychology, 1964, 503–7; R. K. Banks, "Persistence to Continuous Punishment Following Intermittent Punishment Training," 71 J. of Experimental Psychology, 1966, 373–77; R. K. Banks, "Persistence to Continuous Punishment and Nonreward Following Training with Intermittent Punishment and Nonreward," 5 Psychonomic Science, 1966, 105–6; Jan L. Deur and Ross D. Parke, "Resistance to Extinction and Continuous Punishment in Humans as a Function of Partial Reward and Partial Punishment Training," 13 Psychonomic Science, 1968, 91–92. Cf. also the well-known study by A. E. Fisher, referred to by Ross D. Parke, "The Role of Punishment," p. 99.

32. "[O]ne boundary condition . . . is that the punishment has to be introduced in such a way that the goal response is not completely inhibited during acquisition" (Barclay Martin, "Reward and Punishment Associated with the Same Goal Response," 5 Psychological Bulletin, 1963, p. 441).

33. A. Amsel, "The role of frustrative nonreward in noncontinuous reward situations," 55 Psychological Bulletin, 1958, 102–19; "Frustrative Nonreward in Partial Reinforcement and Discrimination Learning: Some Recent History and a Theoretical Extension," 69 Psychological Review, 1962, 306–28; "Partial Reinforcement Effects on Vigor and Persistence," in K. W. Spence and J. T. Spence, eds., The Psychology of Learning and Motivation: Advances in Research and Theory, vol. 1, New York: Academic Press, 1967, pp. 1–65.

34. On this extension of Amsel's stand, and on the experimental corroboration of the extension, cf., e.g., Allan R. Wagner, "Frustration and Punishment," in Ralph Norman Haber, ed., Current Research in Motivation, New York: Holt, Rinehart and Winston, 1966, pp. 229–39; R. K. Banks, "Persistence to Continuous Punishment Following Intermittent Punishment Training," 71 J. of Experimental Psychology, 1966, 373–77; R. D. Parke, J. L. Deur and D. B. Sawin, "The Intermittent Punishment Effect in Humans: Conditioning or Adaptation?" 18 Psychonomic Science, 1970, 193–94; David R. Linden, "Transfer of Approach Responding Between Punishment, Frustrative Nonreward, and the Combination of Punishment and Nonreward," 5 Learning and Motivation, 1974, 498–510.

35. See pp. 10–11 supra.

36. This account differs, of course, from the understanding of internalization by various learning theorists of the neobehaviorist orientation. For instance, Bandura means by the

140

1. LEARNING

term a behavioral change that becomes "partially independent of situational contingencies and outcomes" (*Principles of Behavior Modification*, pp. 617, 624), and explains the partial independence mainly by "one's own system of self-evaluation" (*idem*, pp. 618, 624). In his view the self-evaluatlons, originally generated by extrinsic reinforcements and punishments, operate in a relatively independent way: positive self-evaluations themselves work as reinforcement, and those negative as punishment. Bandura does not define "self-evaluation." What does the expression mean? Apparently some kind of right-wrong experience (cf. *idem*, pp. 32–34, 37–38, 255, 619–22), and if so, his interpretation may be not incompatible with my account. He does not, however, go as far as to admit the existence of specifically moral experiences. Cf. also A. Bandura, *Aggression—A Social Learning Analysis*, Englewood Cliffs, N.J.: Prentice-Hall, 1973, pp. 48–49, 207–13, and 316–18.

37. Various cognitive consistency formulations may be used to explain this persuasive power. Cf., e.g., Charles E. Osgood and Percy H. Tannenbaum, "The Principle of Congruity in the Prediction of Attitude Change," 62 *Psychological Review*, 1955, 42–55.

38. Cf. Jan Gorecki, "Leon Petrazycki," p. 14.

39. H. L. A. Hart, *The Concept of Law*, Oxford: Oxford University Press, 1961, p. 156.

40. This is an empirical statement, and its veracity may therefore be challenged. However, discovery of a society experiencing capricious distributions as being morally right is improbable. True, some religious groups explain various haphazard disasters as morally warranted divine punishments. However, if unable to conceive of any uniform criteria, they assume that the deity, in its incomprehensible wisdom inflicts the punishments on the ground of uniform criteria known only to itself; thus, the punishments are not capricious.

41. H. L. A. Hart, *The Concept of Law*, p. 156.

42. Cf. Part II, Section "Psychological Fallacy: Treatment," *infra*.

43. Cf. text to note 32, *supra*.

44. Exceptionally, however, a mild criminal punishment of an act may be just, even if the act is not experienced as wrongdoing. For instance, some penalties for morally irrelevant offenses against economic regulations are considered as just in various societies, and so are paternalistic penalties imposed on those who harm only themselves (cf. text to note 16, ch. 2, *infra*.) Thus, it is not entirely accurate to treat wrongfulness of prohibited behavior as if it were always a necessary condition for justice of its punishment. (See on this H. L. A. Hart, *Punishment and Responsibility*, New York: Oxford University Press, 1968, pp. 35–40).

45. The most comprehensive functional explanation of the changing views on severity of punishments was offered by Petrazycki. The views evolve largely in an adaptive manner, favoring the needs of the society (cf. text to note 8, *supra*). The better socialized a given society, the less motivational pressure its members need. Thus, primitive societies "need brutal means" (Leon Petrazycki, *Wstep do nauki polityki prawa*, Warszawa: Panstwowe Wydawnictwo Naukowe, 1968, p. 28; original Russian edition appeared in 1896–97). On the other hand, in better developed societies brutal means are not only unnecessary but harmful. That is why, in the course of the development, dominant views react against the excessively severe inherited penalties, and, consequently, the severity itself tends to decline. One of Petrazycki's examples deals with breach of contract: "on the lower levels of culture, various

141

1. LEARNING

threats were being used to ensure scrupulous compliance with the law of contracts, e.g., cutting up the delinquent debtor into pieces by his creditors (the Twelve Tables), selling him into serfdom, public whipping until the debt was paid, doubling the debt in case of delay, etc. The history of the law of contracts displays a decline of pressure; today, there remains only the duty to indemnify for the actually inflicted loss which is not considered a criminal sanction any more'' *(Teoriia prava i gosudarstva v sviazi s teoriei nravstvennosti,* vol. 2, St. Petersburg: Ekateringofskoe Pechatnoe Delo, 1910, p. 524).

46. See on this *Sourcebook of Criminal Statistics 1977,* p. 272–73, Table 2.33. On the protracted divisiveness of the issue, see David B. Davis, ''The Movement to Abolish Capital Punishment in America, 1787–1861,'' 63 *Am. Hist. Review,* 1957, 23–46.

47. Albert Bandura, ''Analysis of Modeling Processes,'' p. 51.

48. Leon Petrazycki, *Wstep do nauki polityki prawa,* p. 40.

49. Albert Bandura, ''Analysis of Modeling Processes,'' p. 51.

50. Cf. text to note 37, *supra.*

51. Jeremy Bentham, *An Introduction to the Principles of Morals and Legislation,* Oxford: Clarendon Press, 1879, p. 184.

52. Cf. Jan Gorecki, ''Social Engineering Through Law,'' in *Sociology and Jurisprudence of Leon Petrazycki,* pp. 121–28.

53. Cf. Johannes Andenaes, *Punishment and Deterrence,* Ann Arbor: University of Michigan Press, 1974, pp. 113–14.

54. Emile Durkheim, *Moral Education,* New York: The Free Press, 1973, p. 167. Cf. also Emile Durkheim, *The Division of Labor in Society,* New York: The Free Press, 1964, chapter 2, esp. p. 108.

55. *Punishment and Deterrence,* p. 114.

Chapter Two: Justice

1. Cf. Weems v. United States, 217 U.S. 349 (1910).

2. Cf., e.g., Penn v. Oliver, 351 F. Supp. 1292 (1972).

3. Herbert Wechsler, ''Sentencing, Correction and the Model Penal Code,'' 109 U. PENN L. REV., 1961, p. 472.

4. For instance, ''in Iowa, burning an empty building could lead to as much as a twenty-year sentence, but burning a church or school carried a maximum of ten; breaking into a car to steal from its glove compartment could result in up to fifteen years in California, while stealing the entire car carried a maximum of ten.'' (Marvin E. Frankel, *Criminal Sentences,* New York: Hill and Wang, 1973, pp. 8–9.)

5. Kenneth Culp Davis, *Discretionary Justice,* Baton Rouge: Louisiana State University Press, 1969, p. 88.

142

6. On the lack of unanimity, see Edwin M. Schur and Hugo Adam Bedau, *Victimless Crimes*, Englewood Cliffs, N.J.: Prentice-Hall, 1974, pp. 59–61.

7. On harsh measures as a proper work incentive for a group at a low level of social development, cf. Jerzy Lande, "The Sociology of Petrazycki," p. 30.

8. Cf. William J. Chambliss, "A Sociological Analysis of the Law of Vagrancy," 12 *Social Problems*, 1964, 67–77.

9. Gilbert Geis, *One Eyed Justice*, New York: Drake Publishers, 1974, p. 222.

10. Cf., e.g., Virgil W. Peterson, *Gambling–Should It Be Legalized?* Springfield, Ill.: Charles C Thomas, 1951.

11. Leviticus 18:22, 20:13.

12. Cf. William Holdsworth, *A History of English Law*, London: Methuen, vol. IV, 1966, p. 504, and vol. XV, 1965, p. 163.

13. An obvious assumption here is: The fact that an otherwise harmless behavior is widely perceived as morally wrong does not itself make the behavior socially harmful. The assumption, challenged by Lord Devlin in his famous essay on *The Enforcement of Morals* (Oxford: Oxford University Press, 1959), was skillfully defended by H. L. A. Hart, *Law, Liberty and Morality* (Stanford, Cal.: Stanford Univ. Press, 1963).

14. *On Liberty*, London: Longmans-Green, 1892, p. 6.

15. H. L. A. Hart, *Law, Liberty and Morality*, pp. 31–32.

16. Legal paternalism, unless narrowly restrained, endangers liberty. That is why the American courts are sometimes inclined to accept it only *sub rosa*. For instance, when upholding motorcycle helmet statutes, they often use reasons other than good of the wearer as justification, like the impact of accidents on the general cost of insurance or the possibility that the cyclist becomes a public charge (cf., e.g., State v. Anderson, 164 S.E. 2d 48 [1968], *affirmed* 166 S.E. 2d 49 [1969]; People v. Newhouse, 287 N.Y. 2d 713 [1968]). However, the sincerity of this stand is dubious: it is hard to believe that the judges are indeed motivated by considerations that seem trivial when compared with harms that endanger the cyclist himself. In the words of Professor Bedau: "Parents force their children to take prudent regard for their own safety in swimming and hiking not mainly because they want to avoid for themselves the cost and nuisance of having to pay for hospitalization, but because they do not want their children encumbered by the injuries which can result from carelessness and inexperience. The advantage to parents and to society generally weighs very small in the balance when compared to the advantages to the children themselves. The same is true of motorcyclists who are required by law to wear protective headgear" (Edwin M. Schur and Hugo Adam Bedau, *Victimless Crimes*, p. 136).

17. *The Wolfenden Report*, New York: Stein and Day, 1963, p. 46.

18. *Ibid.*, p. 44. In 1970, 25 percent of adult Americans did strongly agree, and 23.8 percent did somewhat agree that homosexuality "can cause the downfall of a civilization," Eugene E. Levitt and Albert D. Klassen, Jr., "Public Attitudes Toward Homosexuality: Part of the 1970 National Survey of the Institute for Sex Research," 1/1 *J. of Homosexuality*, 1974, 29–43, p. 34, Table 3.

2. JUSTICE

19. Edwin M. Schur, *Crimes Without Victims,* Prentice-Hall: Englewood Cliffs, N.J., 1965, pp. 110–11.

20. Which, indeed, is the case: according to public opinion polls conducted in 1970 and 1974, the large majority of respondents·(from 77 to 86 percent, depending on the way in which specific questions were asked) considered homosexual behavior as "wrong," "obscene," "vulgar" (E. E. Levitt and A. D. Klassen, "Public Attitudes," p. 31, Table 1, col. 1, 2, and p. 34, Table 3, col. 8; University of Chicago, National Opinion Research Center, *General Social Survey—Spring 1974,* Inter-University Consortium for Political Research, 1975 p. 81).

21. Gilbert Geis, *One Eyed Justice,* pp. 38–39.

22. E. E. Levitt and A. D. Klassen, "Public Attitudes," p. 37, Table 5, col. 5, and p. 40.

23. According to the Gallup Poll of July 1977, 43 percent of Americans felt that "homosexual relations between consenting adults should . . . be legal," 43 percent felt that they should not, and the remainder expressed no opinion (The Gallup Poll, release of July 19, 1977).

24. Merrill A. Needham and Edwin M. Schur, "Student Punitiveness Toward Sexual Deviation," 25 *Marriage and Family Living,* 1963, 227–29.

25. "Modern Medicine Poll on Sociomedical Issues: Abortion, Homosexual Practices, Marihuana," 37 *Modern Medicine* (November 3, 1969), 18–25.

26. *The Wolfenden Report,* p. 48.

27. The Sexual Offenses Act, 1967 (c. 60), Halsbury, 3d ed., vol. 8, pp. 577–82.

28. Evelyn Hooker, "Final Report of the Task Force on Homosexuality," in James A. McCaffrey, ed., *The Homosexual Dialectic,* Englewood Cliffs, N.J.: Prentice-Hall, 1972, pp. 145–55.

29. Edwin M. Schur, *Crimes Without Victims,* p. 79.

30. *Idem,* p. 77.

31. H. L. A. Hart, *Law Liberty and Morality,* p. 22.

32. Cf. Martin Hoffman, *The Gay World,* New York: Basic Books, 1968, pp. 83–87.

33. Peter Wildeblood, *Against the Law,* London: Penguin Books, 1955, p. 61.

34. For instance, "more than a thousand victims paid millions of dollars in extortion money . . . to the . . . members" of a gang that operated, in the 1960s, throughout the United States, and only a small number of them dared to sign complaints. Also "periodic beatings and robbery" of homosexuals are often "carried out on the assumption that the victim will not . . . resort to law enforcement agencies for assistance." (Gilbert Geis, *One Eyed Justice,* pp. 32, 33.)

35. D. J. West, *Homosexuality,* Chicago: Aldine, 1968, p. 54.

36. Cf. text to note 6, *supra.*

37. Cf. the following section.

2. JUSTICE

38. Erich Goode, *Drugs in American Society,* New York: Alfred A. Knopf, 1972, p. 159.

39. Cf. David P. Ausubel, *Drug Addiction,* New York: Random House, 1958, p. 4.

40. Harold Kalant and Oriana Josseau Kalant, *Drugs, Society and Personal Choice,* Ontario: Paper Jacks, Don Mills, 1971, p. 64.

41. Its symptoms include extreme restlessness and anxiety, weakness, depression, insomnia, chilliness alternating with flushing and sweating, spontaneous orgasms, nausea and vomiting, diarrhea, pains in the bones, intestinal and muscle spasms, elevated heart rate and blood pressure, and occasional coma due to cardiovascular collapse.

42. The relative impact of euphoria (as a positive reinforcer) and withdrawal symptoms (as a negative reinforcer) on the chronic effects of opiates is controversial. See on this, e. g., David P. Ausubel, *Drug Addiction,* pp. 20–31; Alfred R. Lindesmith, *Addiction and Opiates,* Chicago: Aldine, 1968; H. Kalant and O. J. Kalant, *Drugs, Society and Personal Choice,* pp. 56–76.

43. Marshall B. Clinard, *Sociology of Deviant Behavior,* New York: Holt, Rinehart and Winston, 1974, p. 393.

44. David P. Ausubel, *Drug Addiction,* p. 37; H. Kalant and O. J. Kalant, *Drugs, Society and Personal Choice,* pp. 81–83; Erich Goode, *Drugs in American Society,* p. 161; National Commission on Marihuana and Drug Abuse, *Drug Use in America: Problem in Perspective,* Washington, D.C.: U.S. Government Printing Office, 1973, p. 141.

45. David P. Ausubel, *Drug Addiction,* p. 13.

46. H. Kalant and O. J. Kalant, *Drugs, Society and Personal Choice,* p. 82.

47. David P. Ausubel, *Drug Addiction,* p. 14.

48. According to a 1958 estimate, approximately 1000 children are born to addicted mothers each year in New York (Gilbert Geis, *One Eyed Justice,* p. 133).

49. David P. Ausubel, *Drug Addiction,* p. 32; H. Kalant and O. J. Kalant, *Drugs, Society and Personal Choice,* p. 28.

50. National Commission on Marihuana and Drug Abuse, *Drug Use in America,* p. 195.

51. The meaning of "guilt" differs here from that in which I used the term when describing the moral experience. There it meant the feeling of wrongfulness of past behavior. Here it denotes the fact that a person who broke a criminal prohibition was able to control his behavior when doing so. The two meanings are related to each other. Those who live in civilized societies do not experience the feeling of wrongfulness of an act unless the actor is able to control his behavior; thus, no one can be guilty in the former sense without being guilty in the latter.

52. Sommerville, J., in Parsons v. State, 81 Ala. 577, 2 So. 854, 858 (1886). These words refer to the "irresistible impulse" doctrine of insanity. I am replacing the expression by "irresistible drive," to avoid the criticism of those who feel that "[t]he term 'irresistible impulse' . . . carries the misleading implication that 'diseased mental condition[s]' produce only sudden, momentary or spontaneous inclinations to commit unlawful acts" (J. Bazelon, in Durham v. United States, 94 U. S. App. D.C. 228, 239 [1954].)

2. JUSTICE

53. Holloway v. United States, 80 U.S. App. D.C. 3, 4–5 (1945); see also Durham v. United States, 94 U.S. App. D.C. 228, 242 (1954).

54. All this does not mean that strict criminal liability could never be justified as a policy measure. However, this may happen only exceptionally, owing to clear and prevailing reasons of general welfare. No such reasons support strict liability of an addict for drug possession and use. Moreover, as the following text should make clear, the liability, once there, brings harmful social consequences.

    For a view close to that expressed in the text, cf. the dissenting opinion by Justice Fortas in Powell v. Texas, 392 U.S. 514 (1968). However, the opinion is dubious. It might have claimed, referring directly to the eighth amendment, that criminal responsibility imposed on anyone for behavior he is powerless to change constitutes cruel and unusual punishment. Instead, the opinion follows Robinson v. California, 370 U.S. 660 (1962). In *Robinson* the Court held as unconstitutional a punishment for being "addicted to the use of narcotics": the state of addiction is a condition not a conduct, and nobody may be punished without *actus reus*. *Robinson,* in the words of Justice Fortas dissenting in *Powell,* stands upon a basic principle: "Criminal penalties may not be inflicted upon a person for being in a condition he is powerless to change" (p. 567). These words constitute a conjunction of two different propositions. First, nobody may be punished just for a condition he is in, without an *actus reus*. Second, nobody may be punished for anything he is powerless to change. Only the first proposition can be found in Robinson. Yet, Justice Fortas wrote the latter into his interpretation of *Robinson,* and then used it as a premise to conclude that addicts must not be punished for possession of narcotics. It would have made better logic to reinterpret directly the cruel and unusual punishment clause of the eight amendment, and thus widen its application, than to stretch the *Robinson* holding beyond its limits.

55. Gilbert Levin, Edward P. Roberts, and Gary B. Hirsch, *The Persistent Poppy,* Cambridge, Mass.: Ballinger Publishing Co., 1975, p. 54.

56. See text to note 47, *supra.*

57. See, e.g., Carl D. Chambers, "Narcotic Addiction and Crime: An Empirical Review," in James A. Inciardi and Carl D. Chambers, eds., *Drugs and the Criminal Justice System,* Beverly Hills, Cal.: Sage Publications, 1974, pp. 130–37.

58. G. Levin, E. P. Roberts, and G. B. Hirsch, *The Persistent Poppy,* p. 54.

59. *Idem,* pp. 52–53.

60. Carl D. Chambers and James A. Inciardi, "Forecasts for the Future: Where We are and Where are We Going" in C. D. Chambers and J. A. Inciardi, *Drugs and the Criminal Justice System,* p. 222.

61. G. Levin, E. P. Roberts, and G. B. Hirsch, *The Persistent Poppy,* p. 54.

62. David P. Ausubel, *Drug Addiction,* p. 69; National Commission on Marihuana and Drug Abuse, *Drug Use in America,* pp. 157–58, 162–63.

63. National Commission on Marihuana and Drug Abuse, *idem,* pp. 171–72.

64. See Part III, Chapter 4, *infra.*

2. JUSTICE

65. Whether it actually does or does not run against the dominant feeling of justice is not known. In the Gallup Poll of 1970 a sample of respondents were asked: ". . . what, in general, you feel should be the jail term . . . for a person caught taking heroin or having it in his possession?" Thirty percent recommended no penalty, medical help, or did not know what to answer, whereas 68 percent opted for punishment (*Sourcebook of Criminal Statistics 1974*, p. 214, Table 2.87). The question was, however, asked in a manner that makes the answers inconclusive for the present considerations. The proper question would have been: "What, if any, should be the punishment for an addicted person caught taking heroin or possessing it only for his use?" For another inconclusive poll, cf. *Sourcebook of Criminal Statistics 1976*, p. 343, Table 2.94.

66. Marvin E. Frankel, *Criminal Sentences*, p. 22.

67. Here again the term "guilt" denotes the experience of past wrongdoing.

68. Florida Statutes, 787.01 (2) and 810.02 (2).

69. Colorado Criminal Code, 18-1-105 (1), 18-3-104 (2), and 18-4-301 (2).

70. U.S. Code, Title 18, Para. 2031.' However, in the wake of *Furman v. Georgia*, 408 U.S. 238 (1971), the section of this paragraph permitting the imposition of the death penalty has been declared unconstitutional, U.S. v. Johnson, 425 F.Supp. 986 (1976).

71. Cf. Section on "Psychological Fallacy: Treatment," *infra*.

72. Marvin E. Frankel, *Criminal Sentences*, p. 21; cf. also pp. 106–7, *idem*.

73. *Idem*, p. 15.

74. "I see no reason why our basic concepts of checks and balances should not apply to . . . passing sentence . . . as well as to procedural matters—complained Judge Craven in U.S. v. Miller, 361 F. Supp. 825, 827.—In no other role can a judge so freely impose a pattern of his personal reactions, philosophy and animosity as when he sentences a man who has no right to appeal though the effect may be his destruction. In no other area of the law are judicial prerogatives so uncontrolled or criteria so obscure."

75. President's Commission on Law Enforcement and the Administration of Justice, *Task Force Report: The Courts*, Washington, D.C.: U.S. Government Printing Office, 1967, p. 23; on similar data from other reports, cf. Kenneth Culp Davis, *Discretionary Justice*, pp. 133–34; Alan M. Dershowitz, "Background Paper" in *Fair and Certain Punishment*, New York: McGraw-Hill, 1976, pp. 103–4.

76. "Countdown for Judicial Sentencing," in *Of Prisons and Justice*, S. Doc. No. 70, 88th Cong., 2d sess., 1964, p. 331 (quoted after Marvin E. Frankel, *Criminal Sentences*, pp. 21–22).

77. *In re* Lee, 177 Cal. 690, 692 (1918).

78. Marvin E. Frankel, *Criminal Sentences*, p. 86.

79. Cf., e.g., Matthew Byrne, Jr., "Federal Sentencing Procedures: Need for Reform," 42 Los Angeles B. Bull., 1967, pp. 563, 567; Ramsey Clark, *Crime in America*, New York: Simon and Schuster, 1970, pp. 222–23; Titus Reid, "A Rebuttal to the Attack on the Indeterminate Sentence," 51 Wash. L. Rev. 1976, 565–606.

2. JUSTICE

80. American Bar Association Project on Minimum Standards for Criminal Justice, *Standards Relating to Sentencing Alternatives and Procedures*, 1968, p. 144.

81. Richard A. McGee, "A New Look at Sentencing," Part II, Federal Probation, September 1974, pp. 5–6.

82. Marvin M. Frankel, *Criminal Sentences*, p. 94.

83. President's Commission on Law Enforcement and Administration of Justice, *Task Force Report: Corrections*, Washington, D.C.: U.S. Government Printing Office, 1967, p. 6.

84. Cf., e.g., E. Barrett Prettyman, Jr., "The Indeterminate Sentence and the Right to Treatment," 11/7 Am. Crim. L. Rev. 1972, pp. 24–25, 29.

85. American Friends Service Committee, *Struggle for Justice*, New York: Hill and Wang, 1971, pp. 88–89; E. Barrett Prettyman, "The Indeterminate Sentence," pp. 25–29.

86. *Struggle for Justice, idem*, pp. 92–93. On an even shorter procedure before the Parole Board in New York, see *Attica*, New York: Bantam Books, 1972, p. 96.

87. Marvin M. Frankel, "Lawlessness in Sentencing," 41 U. Cin. L. Rev. 1972, pp. 9–17. On proceeding of the United States Parole Board, cf. Kenneth Culp Davis, *Discretionary Justice*, pp. 126–30.

88. David A. Ward and Gene G. Kassenbaum, *Women's Prison*, Chicago: Aldine, 1965, p. 20.

89. Edwin H. Sutherland and Donald R. Cressey, *Principles of Criminology*, Chicago: J. B. Lippincott, 1960, pp. 561–62.

90. American Friends Service Committee, *Struggle for Justice*, p. 162.

91. *Idem*.

92. E. Barrett Prettyman, Jr., "The Indeterminate Sentence," pp. 24–25; cf. also Jack Meyerson, "The Board of Prison Terms and Paroles," 51 Wash. L. Rev. 1976, pp. 622–23, note 27.

93. Cf., e.g., President's Commission, *Task Force Report: Corrections*, pp. 62–67; American Friends Service Committee, *Struggle for Justice*, pp. 28–29, 71–76, 92–96; *Attica*, pp. 91–101. Cf. also Bolling v. Manson, 345 F. Supp. 48 (D. Conn. 1972); United States *ex rel.* Sero v. Preiser, 377 F. Supp. 463 (S.D.N.Y. 1974).

94. Sue Titus Reid, "A Rebuttal to the Attack on the Indeterminate Sentence," p. 601.

95. Cf. Sec. 2301 and 2302, Criminal Code Reform Act of 1977 (S. 1437, Report No. 95-605), Washington, D.C.: U.S. Government Printing Office, 1977.

96. For the U.S. district courts cf. *Sourcebook of Criminal Justice Statistics 1977*, p. 562, Table 5.26.

97. *Sourcebook of Criminal Justice Statistics 1977*, p. 144, Table 1.60.

98. *Idem*, p. 164, Table 1.74.

2. JUSTICE

99. On the widespread belief that they should give true answers not only in court but also at an orderly police interrogation, see Erwin N. Griswold, *The Fifth Amendment Today*, Cambridge, Mass.: Harvard University Press, 1955, pp. 56–57; A. Fortas, "The Fifth Amendment," 25 CLEV. B. Ass'n J., 1954, p. 91; Henry J. Friendly, "The Fifth Amendment Tomorrow: The Case for Constitutional Change," 37 U. CIN. L. REV., 1968, 671–726, at 680.

100. White, J., in Brady v. United States, 397 U.S. 742, 750 (1970).

101. See, e.g., estimates by Donald J. Newman, *Conviction—The Determination of Guilt or Innocence Without Trial*, Boston: Little, Brown and Company 1966, p. 3, and by the President's Commission on Law Enforcement and Administration of Justice, *Task Force Report: The Courts*, p. 9.

102. Chief Justice Burger in Santabello v. New York, 404 U.S. 257, 260 (1971).

103. Albert W. Alschuler, "The Trial Judge's Role in Plea Bargaining," 76 COLUM. L. REV. 1976, pp. 1099–1103.

104. Albert W. Alschuler, "The Prosecutor's Role in Plea Bargaining," 36 CHI. L. REV. 50-112, at 111.

105. *Idem,* p. 106.

106. *Idem,* pp. 62–63, 107; Arthur Rosett and Donald R. Cressey, *Justice by Consent*, Philadelphia, J. B. Lippincott Company, 1976, 129–30.

107. His future career may depend on it, the amount of rigidity with which they handle his cases, as well as various favors, like judicial help in collecting fees from his clients, or prosecutorial favors in the discovery process (see A. W. Alschuler, "The Prosecutor's Role" pp. 79–80; A. W. Alschuler, "The Defense Attorney's Role in Plea Bargaining," 84 YALE L. J. 1975, pp. 1225, 1233, 1238–40).

108. See A. Rosett and D. R. Cressey, *Justice by Consent*, pp. 138, 142–43.

109. See Donald J. Newman, *Conviction*, pp. 105–11.

110. Several writers explain plea bargaining by propositions of the theory of bureaucracy; cf., e.g., Abraham S. Blumberg, "The Practice of Law as a Confidence Game," 1/2 L. SOC. REV. 1967, 15–39; Arthur Rosett, "Discretion, Severity and Legality in Criminal Justice," 46/12 S. CAL. L. REV., 1972, 12, 27–29.

111. Cf. Raymond Moley, "The Vanishing Jury," 2/2 S. CAL. L. REV. 1928, pp. 104–9.

112. On specific conditions of their binding force, see text to notes 136–44, *infra.*

113. Santobello v. New York, 404 U.S. 257, 260 (1971). See also opinion of Justice White in Brady v. United States, 397 U.S. 742, 750–52 (1970).

114. Raymond Moley, "The Vanishing Jury," p. 119.

115. On the influence of the defense counsel, see A. Blumberg, "The Practice of Law as a Confidence Game," p. 36, Table 2.

116. Cf. A. W. Alschuler, "The Defense Attorney's Role," pp. 1237–40.

2. JUSTICE

117. For many instances of horizontal overcharging, see A. W. Alschuler, "The Prosecutor's Role," pp. 85–105.

118. Cf., e.g., Para. 52–55 of the German Penal Code, Art. 10, and 66–72 of the Polish Penal Code, Section 34 of the Austrian Penal Act, and Section 62–64 of the Norwegian Penal Code.

119. A. Rosett and D. R. Cressey, *Justice by Consent*, p. 22.

120. Cf. A. W. Alschuler, "The Defense Attorney's Role," p. 1247.

121. A. S. Blumberg, "The Practice of Law as a Confidence Game," p. 29.

122. 272 F. 2d 795 (1st Cir. 1959).

123. Cf. A. W. Alschuler, "The Defense Attorney's Role," p. 1213, note 101.

124. United States *ex rel.* Elksnis v. Gilligan, 256 F. Supp. 244, 254 (S.D.N.Y. 1966).

125. Albert W. Alschuler, "The Trial Judge's Role in Plea Bargaining," pp. 1089–91.

126. A. Rosett, "Discretion, Severity and Legality," p. 26. Cf. also Lloyd L. Weinreb, *Denial of Justice*, New York: Free Press, 1977, p. 83.

127. Cf. A. S. Blumberg, "The Practice of Law as a Confidence Game," pp. 22–23.

128. On some of the abuses, cf., e.g., A. W. Alschuler, "The Defense Attorney's Role," pp. 1194–95, 1223; A. Blumberg, "The Practice of Law as a Confidence Game," pp. 24–25, 29.

129. Cf. A. W. Alschuler, "The Prosecutor's Role," pp. 65–68.

130. Cf. Jon L. Heberling, "Conviction Without Trial," 2 Anglo-Am. L. Rev., 1973, 428, 438; A. W. Alschuler, "The Defense Attorney's Role," p. 1123.

131. Raymond Moley, "The Vanishing Jury," p. 125.

132. Cf. A. W. Alschuler, "The Defense Attorney's Role," pp. 1180, 1210, 1222, 1223, 1313.

133. Santobello v. New York, 404 U.S. 257, 260 (1971); cf. also Justice Stewart's words in Bodenkircher v. Hayes, No. 76-1334, slip. op. at 5-9 (U.S. Supr. Court, January 18, 1978).

134. 397 U.S. 742, 751–52, 753 (1970).

135. Cf., e.g., Kercheval v. United States, 274 U.S. 220 (1926).

136. Brady v. United States, 397 U.S. 742, 754 (1970).

137. *Idem;* McMann v. Richardson, 397 U.S. 759, 768–74 (1970); Parker v. North Carolina, 397 U.S. 790, 794–98 (1970).

138. Brady v. United States, 397 U.S. 742, 755 (1970); cf. also Rule 11 (d) of the Federal Rules of Criminal Procedure.

139. McCarthy v. United States, 394 U.S. 459, 467 (1969); Henderson v. Morgan, 74-1529, slip. op. (U.S. Supr. Court, June 17, 1976).

140. Boykin v. Alabama, 395 U.S. 238, 244 (1970).

141. Santobello v. New York, 404 U.S. 257 (1971). Cf. also United States ex rel. Elksnis v. Gilligan, 256 F. Supp. 244, 249 (S.D.N.Y. 1966).

142. McMann v. Richardson, 397 U.S. 759, 772 (1970).

143. Brady v. United States, 397 U.S. 742, 755 (1970); Parker v. North Carolina, 397 U.S. 790 (1970).

144. North Carolina v. Alford, 400 U.S. 25, 28 (1970).

145. Cf., e.g., A. W. Alschuler, "The Prosecutor's Role," pp. 1247–48.

146. That is why the Supreme Court stresses the weight of defense counsel's presence at plea negotiations (see text to note 137, *supra*), and legislative changes have been recommended to make the negotiations equally available to all defendants and scrutinized by judges (see President's Commission, *Task Force Report: The Courts*, pp. 12–13; American Bar Association, *Standards Relating to Pleas of Guilty*, Approved Draft 1968, pp. 10–12; cf. also American Law Institute, *A Model Code of Pre-Arraignment Procedure*, Tentative Draft No. 5, 1972, p. 62). Some of the recommendations have been embodied in 1974 Amendment of the Federal Rule of Criminal Procedure 11.

147. Cf. A. W. Alschuler, "The Defense Attorney's Role," pp. 1231–36.

148. President's Commission, *Task Force Report: The Courts*, p. 11.

149. Abraham S. Blumberg, *Criminal Justice*, New York: New Viewpoints 1974, p. 89.

150. This does not imply that there would be anything wrong in imposing, on a suspect or witness questioned about a dangerous kind of crime, a legal duty to provide information that he has and in energetically enforcing this duty by criminal penalties in the event of his refusal or misinformation.

151. A. Rosett and D. R. Cressey, *Justice by Consent*, p. 43.

Chapter Three: Certainty

1. FBI, *Uniform Crime Reports 1975*, p. 176, Table 24.

2. The FBI-reported crimes include murder, forcible rape, robbery, aggravated assault, larceny-theft, and motor-vehicle theft.

3. Cf. text to note 2, Introduction, *supra*.

4. Cf. Roger Hood and Richard Sparks, "Citizens' Attitudes and Police Practice in Reporting Offenses," in Israel Drapkin and Emilio Viano, eds., *Victimology*, Lexington, Mass.: Lexington Books, 1974, p. 173.

5. Franklin E. Zimring and Gordon J. Hawkins, *Deterrence*, Chicago: University of Chicago Press, 1973, p. 336.

6. Lawrence A. Friedman, *A History of American Law*, New York: Simon and Schuster, 1973, p. 252.

3. CERTAINTY

7. For a summary of these developments, see Lawrence A. Friedman, *idem*, pp. 248–58.

8. Cf. Wayne R. LaFave, *Arrest: The Decision to Take a Suspect into Custody*, Boston: Little, Brown and Co., 1965.

9. Cf. President's Commission, *The Challenge of Crime in a Free Society*, p. 106; Kenneth Culp Davis, *Discretionary Justice*, pp. 86–87.

10. James Q. Wilson, *Thinking About Crime*, p. 200.

11. Cf. Edwin H. Sutherland, *White Collar Crime*, New York: Dryden Press, 1949, pp. 46–51.

12. James Q. Wilson, *Thinking About Crime*, p. 204.

13. President's Commission, *Task Force Report: Corrections*, p. 27, Table 1.

14. Cf., in particular, American Bar Association, *Standards Relating to Sentencing Alternatives and Procedures*, pp. 72–73; American Bar Association Project on Minimum Standards for Criminal Justice *Standards Relating to Probation* (tentative draft 1970), pp. 1–2.

15. President's Commission, *Task Force Report: Corrections*, p. 27, Table 1.

16. James Q. Wilson, *Thinking About Crime*, pp. 165–66.

17. *Idem*, p. 173.

18. In Lombroso's view, as articulated in the first edition of the *Criminal Man* and never abandoned, criminal behavior is predominantly of organic origin. It is due to atavism—a biological reversion to an earlier stage of evolution, and atavism makes criminal behavior, practically speaking, unavoidable. (Cf. Cesare Lombroso, *Crime: Its Causes and Remedies*, Boston: Little, Brown and Co., 1913, p. 369, and Gina Lombroso-Ferrero, *Criminal Man According to the Classification of Cesare Lombroso*, New York: G. P. Putnam's Sons, 1911, p. 52.)

19. By Charles Goring, *The English Convict: A Statistical Study*, London: His Majesty's Stationery Office, 1913; cf. also Abraham Adolf Baer, *Der Verbrecher in anthropologischer Beziehung*, Leipzig: G. Thieme, 1893.

20. The ways range from Sutherland's "differential association" theory, which attempts to explain all criminal behavior by one condition—contacts with criminal patterns and the following excess of criminal definitions (Edwin H. Sutherland, *Principles of Criminology*, Chicago: J. B. Lippincott and Co., 1955, pp. 74–80), to partial explanations by Sutherland's followers, who consider anyone's contacts with criminal patterns as a factor increasing probability of his criminal behavior (see, e.g., James F. Short, Jr., "Differential Association and Delinquency," 4 *Social Problems*, 1957, pp. 233–39; James F. Short, Jr., "Differential Association as a Hypothesis: Problems of Empirical Testing," 8 *Social Problems*, 1960, pp. 14–25; Marvin L. Voss, "Differential Association and Reported Delinquent Behavior," 12 *Social Problems*, 1964, pp. 78–85). For a more detailed criticism of Sutherland's theory, see my "Crime Causation Theories—Failures and Perspectives," XXV/4 *British J. of Sociology*, 1974, pp. 463–65.

21. Cf., e.g., Sheldon and Eleanor Glueck, *Unraveling Juvenile Delinquency*, Cambridge, Mass.: Harvard University Press, 1951, pp. 108–33.

22. Robert K. Merton's anomie theory is much broader than its restatement used here. The theory focuses on the general conflict between culturally prescribed goals and the social structure that bars many from access to legitimate means for achievement of these goals. Those deprived must reject either the achievement of the goals or the norms prescribing legitimate means. Some reject the latter and resort to deviant behavior to achieve the goals. Some of the others reject both the goals and means and deviate by rebelling against or retreating from the culture (Robert K. Merton, *Social Theory and Social Structure*, pp. 175–248; cf. also Robert K. Merton, "Anomie, Anomia and Social Interaction: Contexts of Deviant Behavior," in Marshall B. Clinard, ed., *Anomie and Deviant Behavior*, New York: The Free Press, 1964, pp. 213–42).

23. *New York Times*, October 6, 1974, Section 4, p. 16.

24. Harry Elmer Barnes and Negley K. Teeters, *New Horizons in Criminology*, Englewood Cliffs, N.J.: Prentice-Hall, 1959, pp. 817–18.

25. Words of Clarence Darrow, quoted after Jessica Mitford, *Kind and Usual Punishment*, New York: Vintage Books, 1973, p. 297.

26. Arthur Lelyveld in *Punishment: For and Against*, New York: Hart Publishing Company, 1971, p. 80.

27. Abraham S. Goldstein and Leonard Orland, *Criminal Procedure*, Boston, Mass.: Little, Brown and Co., 1974, p. 19.

28. President's Commission, *The Challenge of Crime in a Free Society*, p. 1.

29. *Idem*, p. 15.

30. Ramsay Clark, *Crime in America*, New York: Simon and Schuster, 1970, p. 67.

31. Words of Judge Doyle in Morales v. Schmidt, 340 F. Supp. 544, 548 (1972). Cf. also Justice Black's complaint that it is becoming "more and more difficult to gain acceptance for the proposition that punishment of the guilty is desirable" (Kaufman v. United States, 394 U.S. 217 [1969]).

32. For a more formal analysis of social and other determinants of criminal behavior, cf. J. Gorecki, "Crime Causation Theories—Failures and Perspectives."

33. James Q. Wilson, *Thinking About Crime*, p. 52.

34. Harry M. Johnson, *Sociology: A Systematic Introduction*, New York: Harcourt, Brace and World, Inc., 1960, p. 574.

35. Karl R. Popper, *The Open Society and Its Enemies*, vol. 1. Princeton, N.J.: Princeton University Press, 1966, p. 291. Cf. also a more recent, comprehensive statement by James Q. Wilson, *Thinking About Crime*, pp. 43–57.

36. Franz Alexander and Hugo Staub, *The Criminal, the Judge and the Public: A Psychological Analysis*, New York: Collier Books, 1962, pp. 51–52.

37. Karl Menninger, *The Crime of Punishment*, New York: Viking Press, 1968, p. 254.

38. *Idem*, p. 257.

3. CERTAINTY

39. *Idem,* pp. 260, 261.

40. Cf. Section "Inconsistency: Judicial Sentencing Powers . . . ," *supra.*

41. See, in particular, Leslie T. Wilkins, *Evaluation of Penal Measures,* New York: Random House, 1969; Robert Martinson, "What Works? Questions and Answers About Prison Reform," *The Public Interest,* 1974, 22–54, esp. at pp. 29–32.

42. Norval Morris, *The Future of Imprisonment,* Chicago: University of Chicago Press, 1974, p. 17.

43. The learning of criminal attitudes from fellow convicts has been accepted for long and corroborated. Cf., e.g., Frank Tannenbaum, *Crime and the Community,* Boston: Ginn and Co., 1938, pp. 71–81; Donald Clemmer, *The Prison Community,* New York: Rinehard, 1958, pp. 298–313; cf. also Stanton Wheeler, "Socialization in Correctional Communities," 26 *American Sociological Review,* 1961, 697–712.

44. For a closer look at stigmatizing criminals, see Chapter 7, *infra.*

45. Marvin E. Frankel, "Lawlessness in Sentencing."

46. Lloyd E. Ohlin, quoted after James Q. Wilson, *Thinking About Crime,* p. 59.

47. John Bartlow Martin, quoted after Norval Morris and Gordon Hawkins, *The Honest Politician's Guide to Crime Control,* p. 115.

48. Karl Menninger, *The Crime of Punishment,* p. 207.

49. *Idem,* p. 261.

50. James Q. Wilson, *Thinking About Crime,* p. 52.

51. *Struggle for Justice,* pp. 34–47.

52. See, e.g., Ronald H. Beattie and Charles K. Bridges, "Superior Court Probation and/or Jail Sample," Bureau of Criminal Statistics, State of California, Sacramento 1970; Martin A. Levin, "Crime, Punishment, and Social Science," *The Public Interest,* Spring 1972, pp. 96–103. Cf. also conclusions drawn by the American Bar Association from a Florida study conducted in the wake of the post-*Gideon* release of many convicts: "if we today turned loose all of the inmates of our prisons without regard to the length of their sentences and, with some exceptions, without regard to their previous offenses we might *reduce* the recidivism rate over what it would be if we kept each prisoner incarcerated until his sentence expired." (A.B.A., *Standards Relating to Sentencing Alternatives and Procedures,* p. 59.)

53. See, e.g., the excellent analysis of these studies by Robert Martinson, "What Works?" pp. 38–48.

54. T. S. Szasz, *The Myth of Mental Illness,* New York: Harper and Row, 1961, p. 1.

55. Ernest Nagel, "Methodological Issues in Psychoanalytical Theory," in Sidney Hook, ed., *Psychoanalysis, Scientific Method and Philosophy,* New York: New York University Press, 1959, p. 44.

56. Karl Menninger, *The Crime of Punishment,* pp. 185–86.

57. *Idem,* p. 182.

3. CERTAINTY

58. For a judicial criticism of a similar fantasy, see opinions of Justice Francis and Chief Justice Weintraub, in State v. Sikora, 44 N.J. 453 (1965).

59. Cf., e.g., Willard Gaylin and Helen Blatte, "Behavior Modification in Prisons," 13 AM. CRIM. L. REV., 1975, pp. 32–34.

60. See Chapter 1, *supra*.

61. Cf. a cautious defense of their limited use by such writers as Norval Morris, *The Future of Imprisonment*, pp. 25–26, and Richard Delgado, "Organically Induced Behavioral Change in Correctional Institutions," 50 S. CAL. L. REV., 1977, pp. 223–38, 269.

62. Robert Martinson, "What Works?" p. 48.

63. Mapp v. Ohio, 367 U.S. 643, 648 (1961).

64. Elkins v. United States, 364 U.S. 206, 222 (1960).

65. Justice Brandeis quoting James Otis, Olmstead v. United States, 277 U.S. 438, 474 (1928).

66. Coppedge v. United States, 369 U.S. 438, 449 (1962).

67. Bivens v. Six Unknown Federal Narcotics Agents, 403 U.S. 388, 412, 415 (1971).

68. Justice Cardozo in People v. Defore, 242 N.Y. 13, 21 (1926).

69. See Bivens v. Six Unknown Agents of Federal Bureau of Narcotics, 403 U.S. 388, 411 (1971) (Burger, C. J., *dissenting*); Alfred W. Blumrosen, "Contempt of Court and Unlawful Police Action," 11 RUTGERS L. REV. 1957, 526–48.

70. Gilbert v. California, 388 U.S. 263, 273 (1967).

71. 367 U.S. 568, 570–71 (1960).

72. *Idem.*

73. Justice Cardozo in Palko v. Connecticut, 302 U.S. 319, 326 (1937).

74. Watts v. Indiana, 338 U.S. 49, 59 (1949).

75. Brown v. Mississippi, 297 U.S. 278 (1936).

76. The remainder of this section and several paragraphs of chapter 6, part III, *infra*, are adapted from Jan Gorecki, "Miranda and Beyond—The Fifth Amendment Reconsidered." Original Version copyright © 1975 by the Board of Trustees of the University of Illinois. U. ILL. L.F., 1975, 295–312.

77. See Reck v. Pate, 367 U.S. 433, 455 (1961) (Clark, J., *dissenting*).

78. See Culombe v. Connecticut, 367 U.S. 568, 571–74 (1961).

79. Crooker v. California, 357 U.S. 433, 443–44 (1958) (Douglas, J., *dissenting*).

80. See Watts v. Indiana, 338 U.S. 49 (1948); Yale Kamisar, "A Dissent from the *Miranda* Dissents: Some Comments on the 'New' Fifth Amendment and the Old 'Voluntariness' Test," 65 MICH. L. REV., 1966, p. 103.

81. 378 U.S. 1 (1964).

3. CERTAINTY

82. Massiah v. United States, 377 U.S. 201 (1964); White v. Maryland, 373 U.S. 59 (1963); Gideon v. Wainwright, 372 U.S. 335 (1963); Hamilton v. Alabama, 368 U.S. 52 (1961).

83. 378 U.S. 478 (1964).

84. 384 U.S. 436 (1966).

85. P. 468, note 37.

86. United States v. Hale, 422 U.S. 171 (1975); Doyle v. Ohio, 426 U.S. 610 (1976).

87. See Richard H. Kuh, "Interrogation of Criminal Defendants—Some Views on Miranda v. Arizona," 35 FORDHAM L. REV., 1966, 233–42; Note, "Interrogation in New Haven: The Impact of Miranda," 76 YALE L.J., 1967, p. 1576.

88. Miranda v. Arizona, 384 U.S. 436, 542–43 (dissenting opinion).

89. The poll revealed that 68 percent of Americans believe the system of law enforcement does not discourage people from committing crime and that 83 percent believe the police should be tougher in dealing with crime, Sourcebook of Criminal Justice Statistics 1974, p. 188, Table 2.46 and p. 203, Table 2.67.

90. Note "Interrogation in New Haven."

91. Richard J. Medalie, Leonard Zeitz, and Paul Alexander, "Custodial Police Interrogation in Our Nation's Capital: The Attempt to Implement Miranda," 66 MICH. L. REV., 1968, 1347–1422.

92. Lawrence S. Leiken, "Police Interrogation in Colorado: The Implementation of Miranda," 47 DENVER L. J., 1970, 1–53.

93. Some studies are unreliable because of their statistical shortcomings and their use of one-sided data. For example, in a Pittsburgh study almost all data were drawn from police files and information. See Richard H. Seeburger and R. Stanton Wettick, Jr., "Miranda in Pittsburgh—A Statistical Study," 29 U. PITT. L. REV., 1967, 1–26.

94. John Griffiths and Richard E. Ayres, "A Postscript to the Miranda Project: Interrogation of Draft Protesters," 77 YALE L.J., 1967, p. 308; Note "Interrogation in New Haven," pp. 1555, 1578.

95. L. S. Leiken, "Police Interrogation," pp. 27, 30–32; Note "Interrogation in New Haven," p. 1552.

96. J. Griffiths and R. E. Ayres, "A Postscript," pp. 309–10; cf. also Lloyd L. Weinreb, Denial of Justice, p. 124.

97. See L. S. Leiken, "Police Interrogation," p. 31. This adjustive character of the evasions is the reason that many lower courts support apparently illegal police behavior. See Comment, "Waiver of Rights in Police Interrogations: Miranda in the Lower Courts," 36 U. CHI. L. REV., 1969, 413–47.

98. Walter V. Schaefer, The Suspect and Society, Evanston, Ill.: Northwestern University Press, 1967, p. 59.

99. See Edwin N. Griswold, The Fifth Amendment Today, Cambridge, Mass.: Harvard University Press, 1955, pp. 56–57; Abe Fortas, "The Fifth Amendment: Nemo Tenetur Prodere

Seipsum," 25 CLEV. B. ASS'N J., 1954, 91; Henry J. Friendly, "The Fifth Amendment Tomorrow: The Case for Constitutional Change," 37 U. CIN. L. REV., 1968, 671–726, at 680; Charles T. McCormick, "Law of the Future: Evidence," 51 Nw U. L. REV., 1956, p. 222.

100. Miranda v. Arizona, 384 U.S. 436, 504 (1966) (Harlan, J., *dissenting*).

101. S. L. Leiken, "Police Interrogation," pp. 51–52; Note "Interrogation in New Haven," pp. 1545, 1546.

102. J. Griffiths and R. E. Ayres, "A Postscript," pp. 308–9; L. S. Leiken, "Police Interrogation," pp. 24, 51; Note "Interrogation in New Haven," p. 1545.

103. S. L. Leiken, "Police Interrogation," pp. 51–52; Note "Interrogation in New Haven," p. 1545, n. 70.

104. R. J. Medalie, L. Zeitz and P. Alexander, "Custodial Police Interrogation," p. 1378; Note "Interrogation in New Haven," p. 1549, n. 78. One investigation traced a few cases in which innocent suspects might have been convicted because of threats, see Note "Interrogation in New Haven," p. 1546 n. 71 and 1587 n. 177.

105. The authors of the New Haven study concluded that "[d]espite the dark predictions by the critics of the decision, the impact on law enforcement has been small." Note "Interrogation in New Haven," p. 1613.

106. *Idem,* at 1563, 1571.

107. *Idem,* at 1591.

108. *Idem,* at 1594.

109. *Idem,* at 1595 n. 203.

110. *Idem,* at 1608–09. The association between confession or its absence and the outcome of plea bargaining was appraised as at least partially nonspurious.

111. *Idem,* at 1572.

112. *Idem,* at 1571.

113. *Idem,* at 1564, 1574. Some commentators approve of this trend. They believe that egalitarianism demands "placing the inexperienced on a par with the experienced." *Idem,* at 1610. Thus, all criminals, whether bright, stupid, educated, or ignorant, should be treated equally by the system. However, elevating ignorant murderers and rapists to the status of experts in detectional strategy makes a perversion of egalitarianism (see chapter 6, text to notes 15–18, *infra*).

Chapter Four: The Crimes

1. See chapter 1, concluding comments, *supra*.

2. United States v. Moore, 486 F 2d 1139, 1147 (D.C. Cir.), *cert. denied,* 94 S. Ct. 298 (1973).

3. In his dissent from *Moore, idem,* at p. 1260.

4. THE CRIMES

4. Judge Leventhal, concurring in *Moore, idem,* at p. 1160.

5. On the effects of methadone maintenance, *see, e.g.,* Avram Goldstein, "Heroin Addiction and the Role of Methadone in its Treatment," 26 *Archives of General Psychiatry,* 1972, pp. 301–2; James Q. Wilson, Mark H. Moore, and I. Donald Wheat, Jr., "The Problem of Heroin," 29 *Public Interest,* 1972, pp. 24–25.

6. National Commission on Marihuana and Drug Abuse, *Drug Use in America,* p. 321.

7. See James V. DeLong, "Treatment and Rehabilitation," in *Dealing with Drug Abuse— a Report to the Ford Foundation,* 1973, pp. 173–254.

8. See David M. Petersen, "Some Reflections on Compulsory Treatment of Addiction," in James A. Inciardi and Carl D. Chambers, eds., *Drugs and the Criminal Justice System,* pp. 143–69.

9. J. V. DeLong, "Treatment and Rehabilitation," pp. 233–36; see also National Commission on Marihuana and Drug Abuse, *Drug Use in America,* pp. 323–24, and John Kaplan, "A Primer on Heroin," 27 STAN. L. REV., 1975, p. 825.

10. J. Q. Wilson *et al.* "The Problem of Heroin," pp. 22–23.

11. Cf. text to note 15, chapter 2, *supra.*

12. See Edgar May, "Narcotics Addiction and Control in Great Britain," in *Dealing with Drug Abuse—A Report to the Ford Foundation,* p. 345; and William H. McGlothlin and Victor C. Tabbush, "Costs, Benefits, and Potential for Alternative Approaches to Opiate Addiction Control," in J. A. Inciardi & C. D. Chambers, eds., *Drugs and the Criminal Justice System,* p. 80.

13. E. May, "Narcotics Addiction and Control," p. 349.

14. J. Q. Wilson *et al.,* "The Problem of Heroin," p. 18.

15. *Idem.*

16. *Idem.*

17. W. H. McGlothlin and V. C. Tabbush, "Costs, Benefits," p. 104.

18. See E. May, "Narcotics Addiction and Control," pp. 390–91.

19. W. H. McGlothlin and V. C. Tabbush, "Costs, Benefits," p. 100.

20. If a prostitute is a nuisance (e.g., when soliciting in the street), her behavior may be considered socially harmful. If she is not, her activities harm exclusively or predominantly herself. Since the harms do not seem to warrant paternalist sanctions, punishing her is, from a utilitarian standpoint, unfounded. This does not mean that utilitarianism implies neglect of prostitution by criminal law: the harmful, dehumanizing impact of her profession on herself is enough to oppose it by vigorous use of sanctions. The sanctions, however, should be aimed at wrongdoers, not victims. The wrongdoers include all those who knowingly earn by her activities—pimps, brothel keepers, madams, etc. Without their involvement prostitution would not disappear, to be sure, but it would greatly decline.

5. DISCRETION AND BARGAINING

Chapter Five: Discretion and Bargaining

1. The prosecutor may have to retain some amount of well-defined and checked discretion on whether to prosecute for a minor offense; this would resemble the system adopted by various European countries (cf., e.g., Joachim Hermann, "The German Prosecutor" in Kenneth Culp Davis, ed., *Discretionary Justice in Europe and America,* Urbana, Ill.: Univ. of Illinois Press, 1976, pp. 34–46).

2. Cf., e.g., Jan Štěpán, "Possible Lessons from Continental Criminal Procedure," in Simon Rottenberg, ed., *The Econonomics of Crime and Punishment,* Washington, D. C.: American Enterprise Institute for Public Policy Research, 1973, pp. 195–96.

3. The instance was given in text to note 70, chapter 2, *supra.*

4. See text following note 44, chapter 1, *supra.*

5. Cf. *idem.*

6. This is a widespread stand, however difficult its explanation might be; on the explanatory difficulties, cf., e.g., S. Schulhofer, "Harm and Punishment: A Critique of Empasis on the Results of Conduct in the Criminal Law," 122 PENN. L. REV., 1974, 1497–1607.

7. For a recent analysis of some exceptions, see Hans Zeisel and Shari Seidman Diamond, "Search for Sentencing Equality: Sentence Review in Massachusetts and Connecticut," AM. B. FOUND. RES. J., 1977/4, 883–940.

8. Cf., e.g., Weems v. United States, 217 U.S. 349 (1910); Ralph v. Warden, 438 F. 2d 786 (4th Cir. 1970).

9. Cf., e.g., Wilson v. S., 264 So. 2d 828 (Miss. 1972).

10. Marvin E. Frankel, *Criminal Sentences,* p. 85.

11. American Bar Association, *Standards Relating to Appellate Review of Sentences,* p. 7. On a number of similar recommendations made by others, see President's Commission, *Task Force Report: The Courts,* p. 25.

12. American Bar Association, *Standards Relating to Appellate Review of Sentences,* p. 12. For a similar stand, see Marvin E. Frankel, who, when suggesting the review, seems to be concerned only "by cases in which the sentences, though within maximum limits, seem cruelly excessive" (*Criminal Sentences,* p. 82). Also, in view of the President's Commission on Law Enforcement and Administration of Justice, "[t]he most important contribution of appellate review is the opportunity it provides for the correction of grossly excessive sentences" (President's Commission, *Task Force Report: The Courts,* p. 25).

13. Cf. N.C. v. Pearce, 395 U.S. 811 (1969), where the Court pronounced the imposition of a more severe punishment made for the purpose of discouraging appeals as an infringement of due process.

14. See, e.g., J. A. C. Grant, *Our Common Law Constitution,* Boston: Boston University Press, 1960, p. 56; Ernest van den Haag, *Punishing Criminals,* p. 171.

15. Cf. text following note 46, chapter 1, *supra.*

5. DISCRETION AND BARGAINING

16. This brings to mind the limitations for sentence review accepted by the Supreme Court of Pennsylvania in Commonwealth v. Green, 396 Pa. 137; 151 (1959) and by the English Court of Criminal Appeal in Regina v. Ball, 35 Crim. App. 164. On these and related foreign court decisions and statutory norms, see Gerhard O. W. Mueller and Fré le Poole-Griffiths, *Comparative Criminal Procedure,* New York: New York University Press, 1969, pp. 212–17.

17. National Advisory Commission on Criminal Justice Standards and Goals, *A National Strategy to Reduce Crime,* New York: Avon Books, 1975, pp. 368–69.

18. Charles D. Breitel, "Controls in Criminal Law Enforcement," 27 CHI. L. REV., 1960, p. 428.

19. Cf. text to note 9, chapter 3, *supra.*

20. Words of Chief Justice Burger in Santobello v. New York, 404 U.S. 257 (1971).

21. Excessive delays may bring unnecessary hardship to defendants and, sometimes, loss of evidence—after a long time witnesses may become unavailable or their memories may fade. In spite of this, delays—at least delays lasting as long as they do under the present system—are less harmful than often assumed, and that is why I did not discuss them when analyzing the main shortcomings of criminal justice in this country. The assumption of their great harmfulness has a long history: both Bentham and Beccaria believed that prompt application of punishment is a prerequisite for its effectiveness. Later on, the belief has been broadly accepted, especially by those who consider deterrence as the main function of criminal law: "the more closely punishment follows crime, the greater its deterrent value will be; the longer the delay, the smaller the deterrent effect will be . . . upon the offenders themselves and others" (National Advisory Commission, *A National Strategy to Reduce Crime,* p. 327). There is a strong associationist undertone of this widely held conviction: deterrence, if understood as arousal of fear, is perceived as an outcome of association of punishment with the behavior punished, and to evoke the association, punishment must apparently be quick.

This stress on speed does not match the theoretical perspective accepted in this book. The stress would be warranted if the aversion aroused by punishment were mainly (or entirely) due to "automatic" association. The association is "automatic" in animals: as I said earlier, a rat should be punished seconds after behavior X to suppress it. In humans, however, not only the associative process but also awareness of contingencies strongly mediate the response. Speed is therefore less important for arousal of aversion—both moral aversion and aversion that consists in fear. This is particularly true of vicarious punishment: vicarious punishment may arouse aversion in observers irrespective of whether the behavior punished had preceded punishment immediately or some time before (cf. text following note 26, chapter 1, *supra*). Thus, if a wrongdoer gets apprehended many months after commitment of crime, and gets convicted in another year or two, the delay does not impede persuasive instrumental learning on the part of observers as long as they are clearly aware of the link between the crime and the punishment.

22. Henry T. Lummus, *The Trial Judge,* Chicago: Foundation Press, 1937, p. 46.

23. Awareness of this is spreading, and diversion of these acts from the courts is being claimed with increasing frequency. Cf., e.g., President's Commission, *Challenge of Crime*

6. PROVING THE TRUTH

in a Free Society, p. 83; President's Commission on Law Enforcement and Administration of Justice, *Task Force Report: Juvenile Delinquency and Youth Crime*, Washington, D.C.: U.S. Government Printing Office, 1967, p. 16; Norval Morris and Gordon Hawkins, *The Honest Politician's Guide to Crime Control*, pp. 156, 159–60, 166; Edwin M. Lemert, *Instead of Court*, National Institute of Mental Health, 1971, pp. 91–95.

24. Cf. text following note 5, chapter 2, *supra*.

25. President's Commission, *Challenge of Crime in a Free Society;* President's Commission, *Task Force Report: Courts;* President's Commission on Law Enforcement and Administration of Justice, *Task Force Report: Police*, Washington, D.C.: U.S. Government Printing Office, 1967; National Advisory Commission, *A National Strategy to Reduce Crime*.

26. In various parts of the Project on Minimum Standards for Criminal Justice.

27. In the *Model Code of Pre-Arraignment Procedure*, Washington D.C., 1975.

28. This included "the cost for court facilities, clerks, attendants, judge, and jury" (Marcus Gleisser, *Juries and Justice*, New York: A. S. Barnes and Co., 1968, p. 213).

29. *Idem;* Frederic R. Merrill and Linus Schrage, *A Pilot Study of Utilization of Jurors*, Chicago: American Bar Foundation (mimeographed), p. 26; cf. also text to note 96, chapter 2, *supra*.

30. Jerome Frank, *Courts on Trial*, Princeton, N.J.: Princeton University Press, 1973, p. 116.

31. Glanville Williams, *The Proof of Guilt*, London: Stevens and Sons, 1963, p. 271.

32. 1962/63 Harvard Law School Dean's Report, p. 5 (quoted after Harry Kalven, Jr., and Hans Zeisel, *The American Jury*, Boston: Little, Brown and Co., 1966, p. 5 n. 4).

33. Jerome Frank, *Courts on Trial*, p. 132.

34. Duncan v. Louisiana, 391 U.S. 145, 155 (1968).

35. Harry Kalven, Jr., and Hans Zeisel, *The American Jury*, pp. 149–62.

36. Justice Black in Smith v. Texas, 311 U.S. 128, 130 (1940).

37. Patrick Devlin, *Trial by Jury*, London: Stevens and Sons, 1966, p. 164.

38. Duncan v. Louisiana, 391 U.S. 145, 149 (1968).

39. Cf. text to notes 102 and 103, chapter 2, *supra*.

Chapter Six: Proving the Truth

1. A. Fortas, "The Fifth Amendment," pp. 99–100.

2. See, e.g., Wigmore, *Evidence*, § 2251 (McNaughton rev. 1961).

3. W. Schaefer, *The Suspect and Society*, p. 7.

6. PROVING THE TRUTH

4. Ashcraft v. Tennessee, 322 U.S. 143 (1944).

5. Beecher v. Alabama, 389 U.S. 35 (1967).

6. Lynumn v. Illinois, 372 U.S. 528 (1963).

7. See Miranda v. Arizona, 384 U.S. 436, 450–53, 455 (1966). Other police tactics include falsely telling the suspect of his confederate's confession or "reverse line-up" identification by previously coached fictitious witnesses. *Id.* at 453, 455.

8. Sims v. Georgia, 389 U.S. 404, 467 (1967).

9. Darwin v. Connecticut, 391 U.S. 346, 349 (1968); Miranda v. Arizona, 384 U.S. 436, 456 (1966); Haynes v. Washington, 373 U.S. 503 (1963).

10. Miranda v. Arizona, 384 U.S. 436, 450 (1966).

11. Murphy v. Waterfront Comm'n., 378 U.S. 52, 55 (1964).

12. *Idem.* See also A. Fortas, "The Fifth Amendment," p. 98.

13. Cf. Part I, Section "Persuasive Communications," *supra.*

14. This was the Court's position in the "voluntariness" era. See, e.g., Gallegos v. Colorado, 370 U.S. 49 (1962); Culombe v. Connecticut, 367 U.S. 568 (1961); Fikes v. Alabama, 352 U.S. 191 (1957).

15. See, e.g., H. J. Friendly, "The Fifth Amendment Tomorrow," p. 698.

16. *Idem.*

17. See J. Griffith and R. E. Ayers, "A Postscript," pp. 305–6.

18. State v. McKnight, 52 N.J. 35, 52(1968).

19. Some examples of the safeguards inherent in the American legal system are the jury, the executive pardon, and, most importantly, the democratic institutions. If these institutions were to fail, injustice would spread and no procedural safeguards would be of avail. In the McCarthy period the privilege against self-incrimination was called "very nearly a lone sure rock in a time of storm." (E. Griswold, *The Fifth Amendment Today,* p. 173) Indeed, the privilege did help those under abusive investigations. In this case, however, only the democratic institutions, especially the Senate, were able to respond to the political disease and halt the spread of injustice.

20. Miranda v. Arizona, 384 U.S. 436, 467 (1966).

21. See note 29, *infra.*

22. W. Schaefer, *The Suspect and Society,* p. 77.

23. "[T]here will continue to be abuses, so long as it is impossible to know exactly what occurred during the course of interrogation. Enough has been disclosed in reported decisions to establish incontrovertibly the necessity for supervision" (W. Schaefer, *The Suspect and Society,* pp. 37–38).

7. HUMANITARIANISM RECONSIDERED

24. Federal rather than state action has been preferred by some advocates of legislative reform. Federal reform may, however, be constitutionally impermissible. See Note, "Developments in the Law—Confessions," 79 HARV. L. REV., 1966, 935–1119, at 1023.

25. See Miranda v. Arizona, 384 U.S. 436, 526 (Justice White dissenting); American Law Institute, Model Code of Pre-Arraignment Procedure, Tent. Draft No. 6, pp. 26–27.

26. The recording device could begin operating in response to a human voice.

27. Special training is necessary because "most magistrates are either unskilled, . . . or too closely linked with police or prosecutor, or insufficiently mindful of the 'judicial' nature of their role" (Abraham S. Goldstein, "The State and the Accused: Balance of Advantage in Criminal Procedure," 69 YALE L.J., 1960, p. 1168).

28. This practice would remove the obvious objection "that if the police control the equipment, they can turn it on and off when and where it suits their needs" (Paul M. Bator and James Vorenberg, "Arrest, Detention, Interrogation and the Right to Counsel: Basic Problems and Possible Legislative Solutions," 66 COLUM. L. REV., 1966, p. 76).

29. For additional related alternatives, see W. Schaefer, *The Suspect and Society*, pp. 46–49, 76–87; Paul G. Kauper, "Judicial Examination of the Accused—A Remedy for the Third Degree," 30 MICH. L. REV., 1932, 1224–55; Roscoe Pound, "Legal Interrogation of Persons Accused or Suspected of Crime," 24 J. CRIM. L. C. and P. S., 1934, 1014–18.

30. Cf. Note 69, Chapter 3, *supra*.

31. See A. W. Blumrosen, "Contempt of Court," p. 532; Warren E. Burger, "Who Will Watch the Watchman?" 14 AM. U.L. REV., 1964, 9; William Gangi, "Confessions: Historical Perspective and Proposal," 10 HOUST. L. REV., 1973, 1087–1104.

32. Local regulations might, however, require the lawyer's presence as an additional safeguard.

33. See text following notes 13 and 14, chapter 6, *supra*.

Chapter Seven: Humanitarianism Reconsidered

1. Cf. text to notes 32 and 43, chapter 1, *supra*.

2. Cf. text to notes 47–49, chapter 1, *supra*.

3. Edwin M. Lemert, *Social Pathology*, New York: McGraw-Hill, 1951, p. 77; this is a classical articulation of the stand by one of its first architects.

4. Cf. Steven Box, *Deviance, Reality and Society*, London: Holt, Rinehart and Winston, 1971, p. 218; Marshall B. Clinard, *Sociology of Deviant Behavior*, p. 187.

5. Cf. Jan Gorecki, "Crime Causation Theories," pp. 464 and 475, n. 7.

6. Cf. Robert Rosenthal, *Pygmalion in the Classroom: Teacher Expectation and Pupil's Intellectual Development*, New York: Holt, Rinehart and Winston, 1968.

163

7. HUMANITARIANISM RECONSIDERED

7. Cf. note 3, *supra*.

8. Its supporters include, in particular, Howard S. Becker, Kai T. Erickson, John I. Kitsuse, and Edwin M. Schur; its predecessors—George Herbert Mead and Frank Tannenbaum.

9. Emile Durkheim, *Moral Education*, p. 175.

Bibliography

Alexander, Franz and Hugo Staub, *The Criminal, the Judge and the Public: A Psychological Analysis,* New York: Collier Books, 1962.

Alschuler, Albert W., "The Defense Attorney's Role in Plea Bargaining," 84 YALE L.J., 1975, 1179–1314.

Alschuler, Albert W., "The Prosecutor's Role in Plea Bargaining," 36 CHI. L. REV., 1968, 50–112.

Alschuler, Albert W., "The Trial Judge's Role in Plea Bargaining," 76 COLUM. L. REV., 1976, 1059–1154.

American Bar Association Project on Minimum Standards for Criminal Justice, *Standards Relating to Pleas of Guilty,* Approved Draft, 1968.

American Bar Association Project on Minimum Standards for Criminal Justice, *Standards Relating to Probation,* Tentative Draft, 1970.

American Bar Association Project on Minimum Standards for Criminal Justice, *Standards Relating to Sentencing Alternatives and Procedures,* 1968.

American Friends Service Committee, *Struggle for Justice,* New York: Hill and Wang, 1971.

American Law Institute, *A Model Code of Pre-Arraignment Procedure,* Tentative Draft No. 5, 1972 and No. 6, 1974.

Amsel, A., "The Role of Frustrative Nonreward in Noncontinuous Reward Situations," 55 *Psychological Bulletin,* 1958, 102–19.

165

BIBLIOGRAPHY

Amsel, A., "Frustrative Nonreward in Partial Reinforcement and Discrimination Learning: Some Recent History and a Theoretical Extension," 69 *Psychological Review*, 1962, 306–28.

Amsel, A., "Partial Reinforcement Effects on Vigor and Persistence," in K. W. Spence and J. T. Spence, eds., *The Psychology of Learning and Motivation: Advances in Research and Theory*, vol. 1, New York: Academic Press, 1967, pp. 1–65.

Anant, S. S., "A Note on the Treatment of Alcoholics by a Verbal Aversion Technique," 8 *Canadian Psychologist*, 1967, 19–22.

Andenaes, Johannes, *Punishment and Deterrence*, Ann Arbor: University of Michigan Press, 1974.

Anderson, Kenneth E., *Persuasion Theory and Practice*, Boston, Mass.: Allyn and Bacon, 1971.

Asch, Solomon E., "Effects of Group Pressure upon the Modification and Distortion of Judgment," in H. Guetzkow, ed., *Groups, Leadership and Men*, Pittsburgh: The Carnegie Press, 1951, pp. 177–90.

Asch, Solomon E., *Social Psychology*, New York: Prentice-Hall, 1952.

Attica, New York: Bantam Books, 1972.

Ausubel, David P., cf. *Drug Addiction*, New York: Random House, 1958.

Baer, Adolf Abraham, *Der Verbrecher in anthropologischer Beziehung*, Leipzig: G. Thieme, 1893.

Bandura, Albert, *Aggression—A Social Learning Analysis*, Englewood Cliffs, N.J.: Prentice-Hall, 1973.

Bandura, Albert, "Analysis of Modeling Processes," in Albert Bandura, ed., *Psychological Modeling*, Chicago: Aldine, 1971.

Bandura, Albert, "Modeling Theory," in: W. S. Sahakian, ed., *Psychology of Learning: Systems, Models and Theories*, Chicago: Markham, 1970, 350–67.

Bandura, Albert, *Principles of Behavior Modification*, New York: Holt, Rinehart and Winston, 1969.

Bandura, A., E. B. Blanchard, and B. Ritter, "Relative Efficacy of Desensitization and Modeling Approaches for Inducing Behavioral, Affective, and Attitudinal Changes," 13 *J. of Personality and Social Psychology*, 1969, 173–99.

Bandura, A., J. Grusec, and F. L. Menlove, "Vicarious Extinction of Avoidance Behavior," 5 *J. of Personality and Social Psychology*, 1967, 16–23.

Bandura, A. and F. L. Menlove, "Factors Determining Vicarious Extinction of Avoidance Behavior Through Symbolic Modeling," 8 *J. of Personality and Social Psychology*, 1968, 99–108.

Bandura, A. and T. L. Rosenthal, "Vicarious Classical Conditioning as a Function of Arousal Level," 3 *J. of Personality and Social Psychology*, 1966, 54–62.

166

BIBLIOGRAPHY

Banks, R. K., "Persistence to Continuous Punishment Following Intermittent Punishment Training," 71 *J. of Experimental Psychology,* 1966, 373–77.

Banks, R. K., "Persistence to Continuous Punishment and Nonreward Following Training with Intermittent Punishment and Nonreward," 5 *Psychonomic Science,* 1966, 105–6.

Barber, Theodore Xenophon and Karl W. Hahn, "Experimental Studies in 'Hypnotic' Behavior: Physiologic and Subjective Effects of Imaginal Pain," 139 *J. of Nervous and Mental Disease,* 1964, 416–25.

Barnes, Harry Elmer and Negley K. Teeters, *New Horizons in Criminology,* Englewood Cliffs, N.J.: Prentice-Hall, 1959.

Bator, Paul M. and James Vorenberg, "Arrest, Detention, Interrogation and the Right to Counsel: Basic Problems and Possible Legislative Solutions," 66 COLUM. L. REV., 1966, 62–78.

Beattie, Ronald H. and Charles K. Bridges, "Superior Court Probation and/or Jail Sample," Bureau of Criminal Statistics, State of California, Sacramento, 1970.

Bentham, Jeremy, *An Introduction to the Principles of Morals and Legislation,* Oxford: Clarendon Press, 1879.

Berger, Seymour M., "Conditioning Through Vicarious Instigation," 69 *Psychological Review,* 1962, 450, 466.

Berlyne, D. E., *Structure and Direction in Thinking,* New York: John Wiley & Sons, 1965.

Blumberg, Abraham S., *Criminal Justice,* New York: *New Viewpoints,* 1974.

Blumberg, Abraham S., "The Practice of Law as a Confidence Game," 1/2 LAW & SOC. REV., 1967, 15–39.

Blumrosen, Alfred W., "Contempt of Court and Unlawful Police Action," 11 RUTGERS L. REV., 1957, 526–48.

Box, Steven, *Deviance, Reality and Society,* London: Holt, Rinehart and Winston, 1971.

Breitel, Charles D., "Controls in Criminal Law Enforcement," 27 CHI. L. REV., 1960, 427–35.

Brown, R. T. and A. R. Wagner, "Resistance to Punishment and Extinction Following Training with Shock or Nonreinforcement," 68 *J. of Experimental Psychology,* 1964, 503–7.

Burger, Warren E., "Who Will Watch the Watchman?" 14 AM. U. L. REV., 1964, 9.

Byrne, Matthew Jr., "Federal Sentencing Procedures: Need for Reform," 42 L.A. B. BULL., 1967, pp. 563, 567; Ramsey Clark, *Crime in America,* New York: Simon and Schuster, 1970.

Cautela, J. R., "Covert Modeling," paper presented at 5th Annual Meeting of the Association for the Advancement of Behavior Therapy, Washington D.C., September 1971.

BIBLIOGRAPHY

Cautela, J. R., R. Flannery, and E. Hanley, "Covert Modeling: An Experimental Test," 5 *Behavior Therapy*, 1974, 494–502.

Campbell, Donald T., "On the Conflicts Between Biological and Social Evolution and Between Psychology and Moral Tradition," 30 *American Psychologist*, 1975, 1103–26.

Chambers, Carl D., "Narcotic Addiction and Crime: An Empirical Review," in James A. Inciardi and Carl D. Chambers, eds., *Drugs and the Criminal Justice System*, Beverly Hills, Cal.: Sage Publications, 1974.

Chambers, Carl D. and James A. Inciardi, "Forecasts for the Future: Where We Are and Where Are We Going," in C. D. Chambers and J. A. Inciardi, eds., *Drugs and the Criminal Justice System*, Beverly Hills, Cal.: Sage Publications, 1974.

Chambliss, William J., "A Sociological Analysis of the Law of Vagrancy," 12 *Social Problems*, 1964, 67–77.

Clark, Ramsey, *Crime in America*, New York: Simon and Schuster, 1970.

Clinard, Marshall B., *Sociology of Deviant Behavior*, New York: Holt, Rinehart and Winston, 1974.

Clemmer, Donald, *The Prison Community*, New York: Rinehard, 1958.

Comment, "Waiver of Rights in Police Interrogations: *Miranda* in the Lower Courts," 36 U. CHI. L. REV., 1969, 413–47.

Conklin, John E., *The Impact of Crime*, New York: Macmillan, 1975.

Davis, David B., "The Movement to Abolish Capital Punishment in America, 1787–1861," 63 *Am. Hist. Review*, 1957, 23–46.

Davis, Kenneth Culp, *Discretionary Justice*, Baton Rouge: Louisiana State University Press, 1969.

Dawson, Michael E. and William W. Grings, "Comparison of Classical Conditioning and Relational Learning," 76 *J. of Experimental Psychology*, 1968, 227–31.

Delgado, Richard, "Organically Induced Behavioral Change in Correctional Institutions," 50 S. CAL. L. REV., 1977, 215–70.

DeLong, James V., "Treatment and Rehabilitation," in *Dealing with Drug Abuse—A Report to the Ford Foundation*, 1973, 173–254.

Dershowitz, Alan M., "Background Paper," in Twentieth Century Fund Task Force on Criminal Sentencing, *Fair and Certain Punishment*, New York: McGraw-Hill, 1976.

Deur, Jan L. and Ross D. Parke, "Resistance to Extinction and Continuous Punishment in Humans as a Function of Partial Reward and Partial Punishment Training," 13 *Psychonomic Science*, 1968, 91–92.

Devlin, Patrick, *The Enforcement of Morals*, Oxford: Oxford University Press, 1959.

Devlin, Patrick, *Trial by Jury*, London: Stevens and Sons, 1966.

BIBLIOGRAPHY

Durkheim, Emile, *Moral Education,* New York: The Free Press, 1973.

Durkheim, Emile, *The Division of Labor in Society,* New York: The Free Press, 1964.

Fortas, A., "The Fifth Amendment: Nemo Tenetur Prodere Seipsum," 25 CLEVE. B. A. J., 1954, 91.

Frank, Jerome, *Courts on Trial,* Princeton, N.J.: Princeton University Press, 1973.

Frankel, Marvin E., *Criminal Sentences,* New York: Hill and Wang, 1973.

Frankel, Marvin E., *"Lawlessness in Sentencing,"* 41 U. CIN. L. REV., 1972, 1–54.

Friedman, Lawrence A., *A History of American Law,* New York: Simon and Schuster, 1973.

Friendly, Henry J., "The Fifth Amendment Tomorrow: The Case for Constitutional Change," 37 U. CIN. L. REV., 1968, 671–726.

Gangi, William, "Confessions: Historical Perspective and Proposal," 10 HOUST. L. REV., 1973, 1087–1104.

Gaylin, Willard and Helen Blatte, "Behavior Modification in Prisons," 13 AM. CRIM. L. REV., 1975, 11–35.

Geis, Gilbert, *One Eyed Justice,* New York: Drake Publishers, 1974.

Gleisser, Marcus, *Juries and Justice,* New York: A. S. Barnes and Co., 1968.

Glueck, Sheldon and Eleanor, *Unraveling Juvenile Delinquency,* Cambridge, Mass.: Harvard University Press, 1951.

Goldstein, Abraham S., "The State and the Accused: Balance of Advantage in Criminal Procedure," 69 YALE L.J., 1960, 1149–99.

Goldstein, Abraham S. and Leonard Orland, *Criminal Procedure,* Boston, Mass.: Little, Brown and Co., 1974.

Goldstein, Avram, "Heroin Addiction and the Role of Methadone in its Treatment," 26 *Archives of General Psychiatry,* 1972, 291–302.

Goode, Erich, *Drugs in American Society,* New York: Alfred A. Knopf, 1972.

Gorecki, Jan, "Crime Causation Theories—Failures and Perspectives," XXV/4 *British J. of Sociology,* 1974, 461–77.

Gorecki, Jan, "Miranda and Beyond—The Fifth Amendment Reconsidered," U. ILL. L. F., 1975, 295–312.

Gorecki, Jan, "Leon Petrazycki," in Jan Gorecki, ed., *Sociology and Jurisprudence of Leon Petrazycki,* Urbana, Ill.: University of Illinois Press, 1975, 1–15.

Gorecki, Jan, "Social Engineering Through Law," in Jan Gorecki, ed., *Sociology and Jurisprudence of Leon Petrazycki,* Urbana, Ill.: Univ. of Illinois Press, 1975, 115–32.

Goring, Charles, *The English Convict: A Statistical Study,* London: His Majesty's Stationery Office, 1913.

BIBLIOGRAPHY

Grant, J. A. C., *Our Common Law Constitution*, Boston: Boston University Press, 1960.

Griffiths, John and Richard E. Ayres, "A Postscript to the *Miranda* Project: Interrogation of Draft Protesters," 77 YALE L.J., 1967, 300.

Grings, William W., "Verbal-Perceptual Factors in the Conditioning of Autonomic Responses," in: William F. Prokasy, ed., *Classical Conditioning: A Symposium*, New York: Appleton, 1965, pp. 71–89.

Griswold, Erwin N., *The Fifth Amendment Today*, Cambridge, Mass.: Harvard University Press, 1955.

Hart, H. L. A., *The Concept of Law*, Oxford: Oxford University Press, 1961.

Hart, H. L. A., *Law, Liberty and Morality*, Stanford: Stanford University Press, 1963.

Hart, H. L. A., *Punishment and Responsibility*, New York: Oxford University Press, 1968.

Heberling, Jon L., "Conviction Without Trial," 2 ANGLO-AM. L. REV., 1973, 428.

Hempel, Carl G., *Aspects of Scientific Explanation*, New York: The Free Press, 1965.

Hermann, Joachim, "The German Prosecutor," in Kenneth Culp Davis, ed., *Discretionary Justice in Europe and America*, Urbana Ill., Univ. of Illinois Press, 1976.

Hilgard, E. R., R. C. Atkinson, and R. L. Atkinson, *Introduction to Psychology*, New York: Harcourt-Brace-Jovanovich, 1971.

Hirsch, J., "Learning Without Awareness as a Function of Reinforcement," 54 *J. of Experimental Psychology*, 1957, 218–24.

Hoffman, Martin, *The Gay World*, New York: Basic Books, 1968.

Holdsworth, William, *A History of English Law*, London: Methuen, vol. IV, 1966, and vol. XV, 1965.

Hood, Roger and Richard Sparks, "Citizens' Attitudes and Police Practice in Reporting Offenses" in Israel Drapkin and Emilio Viano, eds., *Victimology*, Lexington, Mass.: Lexington Books, 1974.

Hooker, Evelyn, "Final Report of the Task Force on Homosexuality," in James A. McCaffrey, ed., *The Homosexual Dialectic*, Englewood Cliffs, N.J.: Prentice-Hall, 1972.

Humphreys, L. G., "Acquisition and Extinction of Verbal Expectations in a Situation Analogous to Conditioning," 25 *J. of Experimental Psychology*, 1939, pp. 295–301.

Humphreys, L. G., "The Effects of Random Alternation of Reinforcement on the Acquisition and Extinction of Conditioned Eyelid Reactions," 25 *J. of Experimental Psychology*, 1939, 141–58.

170

BIBLIOGRAPHY

Jenkins, W. O. and Stanley, J. C., "Partial Reinforcement: A Review and Critique," 47 *Psychological Bulletin*, 1950, 193–234.

Johnson, Harry M., *Sociology: A Systematic Introduction*, New York: Harcourt, Brace and World, Inc., 1960.

Kalant, Harold and Oriana Josseau Kalant, *Drugs, Society and Personal Choice*, Ontario: Paper Jacks, Don Mills, 1971.

Kalven, Harry, Jr., and Hans Zeisel, *The American Jury*, Boston: Little, Brown and Co., 1966.

Kamisar, Yale, "A Dissent from the Miranda Dissents: Some Comments on the 'New' Fifth Amendment and the Old 'Voluntariness' Test," 65 MICH. L. REV., 1966, 59–104.

Kaplan, John, "A Primer on Heroin," 27 STAN. L. REV., 1975, 801–26.

Kauper, Paul G., "Judicial Examination of the Accused—A Remedy for the Third Degree," 30 MICH. L. REV., 1932, 1224–55.

Kazdin, Alan E., "Covert Modeling and the Reduction of Avoidance Behavior," 81 *J. of Abnormal Psychology*, 1973, 87–95.

Kennedy, Thomas D., "Verbal Conditioning Without Awareness," 84 *J. of Experimental Psychology*, 1970, 487–94.

Kluckhohn, Clyde, *Navaho Witchcraft*, XXII Papers of the Peabody Museum, Cambridge, Mass.: Peabody Museum, 1944.

Kohler, W. *The Mentality of Apes*, New York: Harcourt-Brace, 1925.

Kuh, Richard H., "Interrogation of Criminal Defendants—Some Views on Miranda v. Arizona," 35 Ford. L. REV., 1966, 233–42.

LaFave, Wayne R., *Arrest: The Decision to Take A Suspect into Custody*, Boston: Little, Brown and Co., 1965.

Lande, Jerzy, "The Sociology of Petrazycki," in Jan Gorecki, ed., *Sociology and Jurisprudence of Leon Petrazycki*, Urbana, Ill.: University of Illinois Press, 1975, 23–37.

Leiken, Lawrence S., "Police Interrogation in Colorado: The Implementation of *Miranda*," 47 DENV. L. J., 1970.

Lelyveld, Arthur, *Punishment: For and Against*, New York: Hart Publishing Company, 1971.

Lemert, Edwin M., *Instead of Court*, National Institute of Mental Health, 1971.

Lemert, Edwin M., *Social Pathology*, New York: McGraw-Hill, 1951.

Levin, Gilbert, Edward P. Roberts, and Gary B. Hirsch, *The Persistent Poppy*, Cambridge, Mass.: Ballinger Publishing Co., 1975.

Levin, Martin A., "Crime, Punishment, and Social Science," *The Public Interest*, Spring 1972, pp. 96–103.

Levitt, Eugene E. and Albert D. Klassen, Jr., "Public Attitudes Toward Homo-

171

BIBLIOGRAPHY

sexuality: Part of the 1970 National Survey of the Institute for Sex Research," 1/1 *J. of Homosexuality,* 1974, 29–43.

Liebert, Robert M. and Luis E. Fernandez, "Effects of Vicarious Consequences on Imitative Performance," 41 *Child Development,* 1970, 847–52.

Lindahl, Maj-Britt, "Awareness, Conditioning, and Information Processing in Complex Learning Situations," 14 *Scandinavian J. of Psychology,* 1973, 121–30.

Linden, David R., "Transfer of Approach Responding Between Punishment, Frustrative Nonreward, and the Combination of Punishment and Nonreward," 5 *Learning and Motivation,* 1974, 498–510.

Lindesmith, Alfred R., *Addiction and Opiates,* Chicago: Aldine Publishing Company, 1968.

Lombroso, Cesare, *Crime: Its Causes and Remedies,* Boston: Little, Brown and Co., 1913.

Lombroso-Ferrero, Gina, *Criminal Man According to the Classification of Cesare Lombroso,* New York: G. P. Putnam's Sons, 1911.

Lummus, Henry T., *The Trial Judge,* Chicago: Foundation Press, 1937.

Malinowski, Bronislaw, "Anthropology," *Encyclopaedia Britannica,* 1926, Suppl. I, pp. 132–33.

Marlatt, G. A., "A Comparison of Vicarious and Direct Reinforcement Control of Verbal Behavior in an Interview Setting," 16 *J. of Personality and Social Psychology,* 1970, 695–703.

Martin, Barclay, "Reward and Punishment Associated with the Same Goal Response," 5 *Psychological Bulletin,* 1963, 441–51.

Martinson, Robert, "What Works? Questions and Answers About Prison Reform," *The Public Interest,* 1974, 22–54.

May, Edgar, "Narcotics Addiction and Control in Great Britain," in *Dealing with Drug Abuse—A Report to the Ford Foundation,* 1973.

McCormick, Charles T., "Law of the Future: Evidence," 51 Nw. U. L. REV., 1956, 218–26.

McCord, William, Joan McCord, and Irving Kenneth Zola, *Origins of Crime,* New York: Columbia University Press, 1959.

McGee, Richard A., "A New Look at Sentencing," Part II, *Federal Probation,* September 1974.

McGlothlin, William H. and Victor C. Tabbush, "Costs, Benefits, and Potential for Alternative Approaches to Opiate Addiction Control," in J. A. Inciardi and C. D. Chambers, eds., *Drugs and Criminal Justice System,* Beverly Hills, Cal.: Sage Publications, 1974.

Medalie, Richard J., Leonard Zeitz, and Paul Alexander, "Custodial Police Interrogation in Our Nation's Capital: The Attempt to Implement *Miranda,*" 66 MICH. L. REV., 1968, 1347–1422.

172

BIBLIOGRAPHY

Melamed, Barbara G. and Lawrence J. Siegel, "Reduction of Anxiety in Children Facing Hospitalization and Surgery by Use of Filmed Modeling," 43 *J. of Consulting and Clinical Psychology*, 1975, 511–21.

Menninger, Karl, *The Crime of Punishment*, New York: The Viking Press, 1968.

Merrill, Frederic R. and Linus Schrage, *A Pilot Study of Utilization of Jurors*, Chicago: American Bar Foundation (mimeographed).

Merton, Robert K., "Anomie, Anomia and Social Interaction: Contexts of Deviant Behavior," in Marshall B. Clinard, ed., *Anomie and Deviant Behavior*, New York: The Free Press, 1964.

Merton, Robert K., *Social Theory and Social Structure*, New York: Free Press, 1968.

Meyerson, Jack, "The Board of Prison Terms and Paroles and Indeterminate Sentencing: A Critique," 51 Wash. L. Rev., 1976, 617–30.

Mill, J. S., *On Liberty*, London: Longmans-Green, 1892.

Miller, N. E., "Learning of Visceral and Glandular Responses," 163 *Science*, 1969, 434–45.

Mitford, Jessica, *Kind and Usual Punishment*, New York, Vintage Books, 1973.

"Modern Medicine Poll on Sociomedical Issues: Abortion, Homosexual Practices, Marihuana," 37 *Modern Medicine* (November 3, 1969), 18–25.

Moley, Raymond, "The Vanishing Jury," 2/2 S. Cal. L. Rev., 1928, 97–127.

Morris, Norval, *The Future of Imprisonment*, Chicago: University of Chicago Press, 1974.

Morris, Norval and Gordon Hawkins, *The Honest Politician's Guide to Crime Control*, Chicago: University of Chicago Press, 1969.

Mueller Gerhard O. W. and Fré le Poole-Griffiths, *Comparative Criminal Procedure*, New York: New York University Press, 1969.

Nagel, Ernest, "A Formalization of Functionalism," in *Logic Without Metaphysics*, Glencoe, Ill.: The Free Press, 1956.

Nagel, Ernest, "Methodological Issues in Psychoanalytical Theory," in Sidney Hook, ed., *Psychoanalysis, Scientific Method and Philosophy*, New York: New York University Press, 1959, pp. 38–56.

Nagel, Ernest, *The Structure of Science*, New York: Harcourt, Brace and World, Inc., 1961.

National Commission on Marihuana and Drug Abuse, *Drug Abuse in America: Problem in Perspective*, Washington, D.C.: U.S. Government Printing Office, 1973.

National Advisory Commission on Criminal Justice Standards and Goals, *A National Strategy to Reduce Crime*, New York: Avon Books, 1975.

Needham, Merrill A. and Edwin M. Schur, "Student Punitiveness Toward Sexual Deviation," 25 *Marriage and Family Living*, 1963.

BIBLIOGRAPHY

Newman, Donald J., *Conviction—The Determination of Guilt or Innocence Without Trial,* Boston: Little, Brown and Company, 1966.

Note, "Development in the Law—Confessions," 79 HARV. L. REV., 1966, 935–1119.

Note, "Interrogation in New Haven: The Impact of *Miranda,*" 76 YALE L.J., 1967, 1519–1648.

O'Connor, R. D., "Modification of Social Withdrawal Through Symbolic Modeling," 2 *Journal of Applied Behavioral Analysis,* 1969, 15–22.

Osgood, Charles E. and Percy H. Tannenbaum, "The Principle of Congruity in the Prediction of Attitude Change," 62 *Psychological Review,* 1955, 42–55.

Ossowska, Maria, *Social Determinants of Moral Ideas,* London: Routledge and Kegan Paul, 1971.

Parke, Ross D., "The Role of Punishment in the Socialization Process," in Ronald A. Hoppe, G. Alexander Milton, and Edward S. Simmel, eds., *Early Experiences in the Process of Socialization,* New York: Academic Press, 1970.

Parke, Ross D., ed., *Recent Trends in Social Learning Theory,* New York: Academic Press, 1972.

Parke, R. D., J. L. Deur, and D. B. Sawin, "The Intermittent Punishment Effect in Humans: Conditioning or Adaptation?" 18 *Psychonomic Science,* 1970, 193–94.

Peterson, David M., "Some Reflections on Compulsory Treatment of Addiction," in Carl D. Chambers and James A. Inciardi, eds., *Drugs and the Criminal Justice System,* Beverly Hills, Cal.: Sage Publications, 1974.

Petersen, Virgil W., *Gambling—Should It Be Legalized?* Springfield, Ill.: Charles C Thomas, 1951.

Petrazycki, Leon, *Law and Morality,* Cambridge, Harvard University Press, 1955.

Petrazycki, Leon, *Wstep do nauki polityki prawa,* Warszawa: Panstwowe Wydawnictwo Naukowe, 1968.

Petrazycki, Leon, *Teoriia prava i gosudarstva v sviazi s teoriei nravstvennosti,* vol. 2, St. Petersburg: Ekateringofskoe Pechatnoe Delo, 1910.

Philbrick, D. B., and L. Postman, "A Further Analysis of 'Learning Without Awareness,' " 68 *American J. of Psychology,* 1955, 417–24.

Popper, Karl R., *The Open Society and Its Enemies,* vol. I. Princeton, N.J.: Princeton University Press, 1966.

Postman, L., and J. Sassenrath, "The Automatic Action of Verbal Rewards and Punishments," 65 *J. of General Psychology,* 1961, 109–36.

Pound, Roscoe, "Legal Interrogation of Persons Accused or Suspected of Crime," 24 J. CRIM. L.C. and P.S. 1934, 1014–18.

174

BIBLIOGRAPHY

Prettyman, E. Barrett, Jr., "The Indeterminate Sentence and the Right to Treatment," 11/7 AM. CRIM. L. REV., 1972, 7–37.

President's Commission on Law Enforcement and Administration of Justice, *Task Force Report: The Courts,* Washington, D.C.: U.S. Government Printing Office, 1967.

President's Commission on Law Enforcement and Administration of Justice, *Task Force Report: Corrections,* Washington, D.C.: U.S. Government Printing Office, 1967.

President's Commission on Law Enforcement and Administration of Justice, *Task Force Report: Juvenile Delinquency and Youth Crime,* Washington, D.C.: U.S. Government Printing Office, 1967.

President's Commission on Law Enforcement and Administration of Justice, *Task Force Report: Police,* Washington, D.C.: U.S. Government Printing Office, 1967.

President's Commission on Law Enforcement and Administration of Justice, *The Challenge of Crime in a Free Society,* Washington, D.C.: U.S. Government Printing Office, 1967.

Rachman, S., "Clinical Applications of Observational Learning, Imitation and Modeling," 3 *Behavior Therapy,* 1972, 379–97.

Reid, Titus, "A Rebuttal to the Attack on the Indeterminate Sentence," 51 WASH. L. REV., 1976, 565–606.

Renner, K. E., "Delay of Reinforcement: A Historical Review," 61 *Psychological Bulletin,* 1964, 341–61.

Rosenthal, Robert, *Pygmalion in the Classroom: Teacher Expectation and Pupil's Intellectual Development,* New York: Holt, Rinehart and Winston, 1968.

Rosett, Arthur, "Discretion, Severity and Legality in Criminal Justice," 46/12 S. CAL. L. REV., 1972, 12–29.

Rosett, Arthur and Donald R. Cressey, *Justice by Consent,* Philadelphia, J. B. Lippincott Company, 1976.

Sassenrath, J. M., "Transfer of Learning Without Awareness," 10 *Psychological Reports,* 1962, 411–20.

Schaefer, Walter V., *The Suspect and Society,* Evanston, Ill.: Northwestern University Press, 1967.

Schulhofer, S., "Harm and Punishment: A Critique of Emphasis on the Results of Conduct in the Criminal Law," 122 U. PENN. L. REV., 1974, 1497–1607.

Schur, Edwin M., *Crimes Without Victims,* Englewood Cliffs, N.J.: Prentice-Hall, 1965.

Schur, Edwin M. and Hugo Adam Bedau, *Victimless Crimes,* Englewood Cliffs, N.J.: Prentice-Hall, 1974.

BIBLIOGRAPHY

Sears, Robert R., Eleanor E. Maccoby, and Harry Levin, *Patterns of Child Rearing*, White Plains, N.Y.: Row, Peterson, 1957.

Seeburger, Richard H. and R. Stanton Wettick, Jr., *"Miranda* in Pittsburgh—A Statistical Study," 29 U. PITT. L. REV., 1967, 1–26.

Short, James F., Jr., "Differential Association as a Hypothesis: Problems of Empirical Testing," 8 *Social Problems,* 1960, 14–25.

Short, James F., Jr., "Differential Association and Delinquency," 4 *Social Problems,* 1957, 233–39.

Štěpán, Jan, "Possible Lessons from Continental Criminal Procedure," in Simon Rottenberg, ed., *The Economics of Crime and Punishment,* Washington D.C., American Enterprise Institute for Public Policy Research, 1973.

Stotland, Ezra, "Explanatory Investigations of Empathy," in L. Berkowitz, ed., *Advances in Experimental Social Psychology,* vol. 4, New York: Academic Press 1969, pp. 288–97.

Sutherland, Edwin H., *Principles of Criminology,* Chicago: J. B. Lippincott, 1955.

Sutherland, Edwin H., *White Collar Crime,* New York: Dryden Press, 1949.

Sutherland, Edwin H., and Donald R. Cressey, *Principles of Criminology,* Chicago: J. B. Lippincott, 1960.

Szasz, T. S. *The Myth of Mental Illness,* New York, Harper and Row, 1961.

Tannenbaum, Frank, *Crime and the Community,* Boston: Ginn and Co., 1938.

Thaver, F., and W. F. Oakes, "Generalization and Awareness in Verbal Operant Conditioning," 6 *J. of Personality and Social Psychology,* 1967, 391–9.

University of Chicago, National Opinion Research Center, *General Social Survey—Spring 1974,* Inter-University Consortium for Political Research, 1975.

Van den Haag, Ernest, *Punishing Criminals,* New York: Basic Books, 1975.

Voss, Marvin L., "Differential Association and Reported Delinquent Behavior," 12 *Social Problems,* 1964.

Wagner, Allan R., "Frustration and Punishment," in Ralph Norman Haber, ed., *Current Research in Motivation,* New York: Holt, Rinehart and Winston, 1966, pp. 229–39.

Walters, Richard W., Marion Leat, and Louis Mezei, "Inhibition and Disinhibition of Responses Through Empathetic Learning," 17 *Canadian J. of Psychology,* 1963, 235–43.

Ward, David A. and Gene G. Kassenbaum, *Women's Prison,* Chicago: Aldine, 1965.

Wechsler, Herbert, "Sentencing, Correction and the Model Penal Code," U. PENN. L. REV., 1961, 465–93.

Weinreb, Lloyd L., *Denial of Justice,* New York: Free Press, 1977.

West, D. J., *Homosexuality,* Chicago: Aldine, 1968.

BIBLIOGRAPHY

Wheeler, Stanton, "Socialization in Correctional Communities," 26 *American Sociological Review*, 1961, 697–712.

Wigmore, *Evidence*, Vol. 8 (McNaughton rev.), 1961.

Wildeblood, Peter, *Against the Law*, London: Penguin Books, 1955.

Wilkins, Leslie, *Evaluation of Penal Measures*, New York: Random House, 1969.

Williams, Glanville, *The Proof of Guilt*, London: Stevens and Sons, 1963.

Wilson, James Q., *Thinking About Crime*, New York: Basic Books, 1975.

Wilson, James Q., Mark H. Moore, and I. Donald Wheat, "The Problem of Heroin," 29 *Public Interest*, 1972, 3–31.

Wolfenden Report, New York: Stein and Day, 1963.

Zeisel, Hans and Shari Seidman Diamond, "Search for Sentencing Equality: Sentence Review in Massachusetts and Connecticut," Am. B. Found. Res. J., 1977/4, 883–940.

Zimring, Franklin E. and Gordon J. Hawkins, *Deterrence*, Chicago: University of Chicago Press, 1973.

Index

179

INDEX

Burger, Chief Justice Warren E.: on plea bargaining, 52; on exclusionary rule, 82

Capital punishment, 24

Capriciousness, *see* Consistency and inconsistency of criminal punishments

Causes of crime, *see* Explanation of criminal behavior

Certainty of criminal punishment: as a prerequisite for moral learning, 13-16, 19, 22-23, 24, 27, 89, 93; and discretion, 32-33, 59, 64-67, 103; and rehabilitation, 44-45, 67, 74, 76-77, 81; and plea bargaining, 59; as a utopian ideal, 63; its lack in the United States, 63-64, 67, 71, 81, 103; and leniency, 64-67; and constitutional constraints, 64, 81-89; arguments against, 67-71, 109-10, 127-28; and exclusionary rule, 81; and *Miranda* warnings, 87-89; and legislative recommendations, 93, 103-5, 109; and drug dealers, 98

Classical conditioning, 16

Classical school of criminology, 67-68, 69

Cognitive processes, *see* Instrumental learning

Communications, *see* Persuasive communications

Community correctional programs, *see* Rehabilitation

Confessions, 83-89, 117-26; and evidence, 83, 86, 88, 117; voluntariness of, 84-85, 125; and certainty of punishment, 86, 87-89, 117; and plea bargaining, 88-89; as a cost-cutting device, 115, 117

Consistency and inconsistency of criminal punishment: defined, 21-22; and justice, 21-22, 23, 24, 31, 32-33, 46-47, 48-49, 59-60; and discretion, 32-33, 44, 45-47, 59, 103; and lawmakers' blunders, 32, 142 *n*.4; and indeterminate sentences, 44, 48-49; and plea bargaining, 50, 59-60; and *Miranda* warnings, 89; and arguments against consistency, 67-71

Costs of crime, xi-xii

Costs of criminal justice administration, xii; and need to economize, 50, 109-10; and plea

bargaining, 50-51; ways of cutting, 109-14; and confessions, 115, 117

Counseling, *see* Rehabilitation, Prisons

Counteraction, psychological, 5, 136 *n*.1

Courts: lower, overload and need to decongest, 33, 111, 112; need for unification and management improvements, 112

Craven, Judge: on judicial discretion, 147 *n*.74

Crime rates, xi

Criminal punishment as an implement of learning, 22-27, 73, 127, 132-33; general society as its addressee, xiii, 3, 22, 44-45, 80-81, 108-9, 131; prerequisites for effectiveness, xiii-xiv, 22-27; and its certainty, 22-23, 24, 27, 63, 68, 89, 93; and its intermittence, 23, 59, 63-67, 71, 81, 103; and its persuasiveness, 23, 38, 43, 61-62, 103, 108-9; and its justice, 23-25, 38, 43, 60-62, 81, 93; and its consistency, 24, 31, 32-33, 46-47, 48-49, 60-62, 93; and its severity, 24-25, 68, 129; its secondary role, 26-27; its limitations, 26-27, 93; and unjust selection of criminal behavior, 31-32, 38, 43; and delay, 160 *n*.21

Culombe v. Connecticut, 83

Cultural evolution: and severity of punishments, 24, 141-42 *n*.45; and selection of punishable behavior, 31-32, 34-35; and standards of procedural fairness, 119-20

Dante Alighieri, 19

Defense counsel, *see* Police interrogation

Delay: of punishment, 13, 160 *n*.21; in court, 160 *n*.21

Determinism, 69, 74

Deterrence, general, xiv, 25, 73, 77, 93, 109, 129, 132, 160 *n*.21

Devlin, Lord: on jury 113-14; on punishment of immortality, 143 *n*.13

Differential association theory, 69, 152 *n*.20

Discretion: and inconsistency of punishments, 32-34, 44, 45-47, 59; of police, 32-33, 64, 65-66, 67, 103-4; of prosecutors, 32-33, 64, 65, 66, 104-5, 109, 159 *n*.1; of parole boards, 32-33, 47-49; as a prerequisite for justice, 44; of juries, 44, 65; and cruelty of

INDEX

INDEX

Prisons (*Continued*)
and Patuxent, 47-48; movement to abolish, 70-71, 76; demoralizing influence of, 75, 76, 77, 128, 129; psychotherapy and counseling in, 75-76, 129

Privilege against self-incrimination: and procedural fairness, 82, 118-20, 122; and comment at trial on the suspect's silence, 84, 125; and its application to the states, 85; and its extension to interrogation, 85-86; as an ultimate value, 118; and protecting the innocent, 118, 122; and equal protection, 121, 122, 157 *n*.113; and unjust laws, 121-22; and democratic institutions, 162 *n*.19. *See also* Confessions, *Miranda* warnings, Police interrogation

Probation, 66-67, 77, 105

Prognosis by judges and parole authorities, 44, 45, 48

Prosecutor, *see* Discretion, plea bargaining

Prostitution, 34, 101, 110, 111, 158 *n*.20

Provocation, psychological, 5, 136 *n*.1

Psychoanalysis, 68-69, 74-75, 77-79, 80

Psychotherapy, 74-75, 77, 80, 97. *See also* rehabilitation of criminals

Punishment: severity of, 13, 15, 19, 23, 24-25, 31, 32, 44-47, 59-60, 105, 107-8, 129; in common and professional languages, 10-11, 17-18; direct, 11, 18-19; vicarious, 11-13, 18-19, 22-23; timing of, 13, 19, 160 *n*.21; scheduling of, 13-16, 19, 22-23, 24, 59, 63-67; delayed, 13, 110, 160 *n*.21; of instrumental response, 13-15, 16; of extreme power, 15, 23, 129; consisting in nonreward, 16; and classical conditioning, 16; cruel, 23, 24, 25, 31, 32, 33, 38, 49, 76; capital, 24; of harmless behavior, 33-43; negotiated, 59-62; criticism of, 69-71, 74-75, 76; summary, 112; and stigma, 129-31. *See also* Certainty of criminal punishment, Consistency and inconsistency of criminal punishment, Criminal punishment as an implement of learning, Indeterminate sentences, Instrumental learning, Justice and injustice

Puritanism, 34-35

Quakers, xiii, 75

Rehabilitation of criminals: belief in, xiv, 44, 47, 74-75; and certainty of punishment, 44, 45, 67, 76-77, 81; and judicial discretion, 45, 67, 75, and prognosis, 45, 48; and indeterminate sentences, 47, 75; and leniency, 67, 74-81; and antipunitive philosophy, 74-81; and psychoanalysis, 74-79; ineffectiveness of, 75-76, 77-80, 129; and lack of a viable theory, 77-78; and behavior modification, 79-80; and chemotherapy, 79-80; and psychosurgery, 79-80; harmful influence of, 81

Reinforcement: scheduling of, 9-16, 19; vicarious, defined, 11; intensity of, 13, 19; timing of, 13, 19; and drug abuse, 39. *See also* Instrumental learning

Retribution, 74

Review of sentences, *see* Criminal sentences

Rolleston Committee, 99

Schaefer, Walter V.: on interrogations, 162 *n*.23

Schur, Edwin M.: on legal paternalism, 143 *n*.16

Severity of punishment, *see* Criminal punishment as an implement of learning, punishment

Socrates, 4, 20, 27

Social problems: as outcome of criminal behavior, xi-xiii, 73-74, 127, 133; as explanation of criminal behavior, xiv, 69-73; as concerns independent of criminal behavior, 71

Soviet criminology, 72

Stigma: and criminal self-image, 128; criminogenic impact of, 76, 128, 130; and juvenile delinquency, 128; and "labeling perspective," 130-31; adaptive role of, 131

Strict liability, 146 *n*.54

Sutherland, Edwin H.: on differential association, 152 *n*.20

Tarde, Gabriel, 68

Totalitarianism: and arrest of communications,